THE COMPLETE GUIDE TO

Canning

Created and designed
by the editorial staff
of Ortho Books

Edited by
Susan M. Lammers

Written by
Charlotte Walker Pisinski

Designed by
James Stockton

Photography by
Michael Lamotte

Photo Styling by
Sara Slavin

Ortho Books

Publisher
Robert L. Iacopi

Editorial Director
Min S. Yee

Managing Editor
Anne Coolman

Horticultural Editor
Michael D. Smith

Senior Editors
Kenneth R. Burke
Sally W. Smith

Production Manager
Laurie S. Blackman

Horticulturist
Michael D. McKinley

Associate Editors
Barbara J. Ferguson
Julia W. Hall
Susan M. Lammers

Production Assistant
Darcie S. Furlan

National Sales Manager
Garry P. Wellman

Distribution/Operations
Supervisor
William T. Pletcher

Operations Assistant
Donna M. White

Administrative Assistant
Georgiann Wright

Address all inquiries to:
Ortho Books
Chevron Chemical Company
Consumer Products Division
575 Market Street
San Francisco, CA 94105

First Printing in March 1982.

1 2 3 4 5 6 7 8 9

82 83 84 85 86 87

ISBN 0-89721-003-4

Library of Congress Catalog Card
Number 81-86184

Chevron Chemical Company
575 Market Street, San Francisco, CA 94105

Front Cover: Pantry shelves laden
with home canned fruits, preserves,
pickles and chutneys make a bountiful
display. The canning equipment
shown is standard in most kitchens.

Back Cover: Fresh fruits, berries,
and vegetables are just a few of the
items that can be preserved for later
enjoyment.

Title Page: Writer/Home Economist,
Charlotte Walker Pisinski wraps up a
few of her favorite canned items to
give as gifts to friends and family. See
"Specialities of the House" page 85
for gift wrapping ideas and recipes
for Charlotte's gourmet favorites.

Acknowledgements:

Recipe Consultant:
Olivia Erschen
Fairfax, CA

Recipe Tester:
Margaret L. Kneller
San Francisco, CA

Front Cover Photogapher:
Fred Lyon

Illustrator:
Ellen Blonder
Mill Valley, CA

Typography:
Turner, Brown & Yeoman, Inc.
San Francisco, California

Color Separations:
Colorscan
Palo Alto, California

Copyediting:
Editcetera
Berkeley, California

We also thank the following individuals
and organizations for
their contributions to this book:

Amana Refrigeration Inc.
Amana, Iowa

Ball Corporation
Muncie, Indiana

California Brandy Advisory Board
San Francisco, CA

California Tree Fruit Commission
Sacramento, CA

Marge Childress
San Anselmo, CA

Jaunita Erschen
Dubuque, Iowa

Daryl and Margie Hurst
Twin Hill Ranch
Sebastopol, CA

Judith L. Imhoff
San Francisco, CA

Fran Irwin
San Francisco, CA

Virginia Ladensohn
San Francisco, CA

University of California
Extension Service
Davis, CA

United States Department
of Agriculture
Washington, D.C.

THE COMPLETE GUIDE TO

Canning

The Art and Science of Canning and Pickling

A Short Course on Canning

Jellies, Jams, and Other Fruit Preserves

Canning Fruits, Tomatoes, and Juices

Canning Vegetables, Meats, and Poultry

All About Pickling

Specialities of the House

The Art and Science of Canning and Pickling

Two ancient methods of food preservation—canning and pickling—now are modern culinary feats practiced and enjoyed by everyone, whether you have a garden or not. Here's the firsthand "how-to" guide to filling your pantry.

Canning and pickling capture nature's bounty at its peak of perfection and preserve it for later enjoyment. The discovery of these preserving methods helped free the human diet from the limitations of seasonal cycles. The bounty of spring and summer could be preserved and enjoyed through the meager months of winter.

The art of pickling predates written history. Its roots go deep into the Chinese culture. It's also known that Cleopatra valued pickles as a secret of beauty and health. She introduced pickling to Julius Caesar, who added these foods to the daily diets of the Roman legions and gladiators to help keep his men in top physical condition.

Gradually, the passion for pickles spread throughout Europe and then west to America. Early explorers of this continent carried kegs of sauerkraut and pickles with them across the ocean and ate them to prevent scurvy, a disease caused by vitamin C deficiency. The American continent was even named af-

Herb vinegars, pickled fruits and vegetables, relishes, and crystal-clear jellies and marmalades create a colorful display.

ter a Spanish pickle dealer, Amerigo Vespucci.

Pickling was also an important method of preservation in the American colonies. Early puritan settlers believed that pickles should be served daily as a "sour" reminder to be thankful for the "sweet" gifts of the land.

Canning is a relatively recent invention. In 1809, after 14 years of experiments, Nicolas Appert, a Parisian confectioner and distiller, fathered the process of preserving food in glass bottles by sealing the bottles with cork and gradually heating them. His discovery was prompted by the French government's offer of a 12,000 franc prize for the discovery of a way to preserve food so that it could be transported long distances to the armies of the Revolution.

The success of Appert's preserving method relied on containing food in an airtight jar, and then heating the filled jar to inactivate and destroy the spoilage organisms that cause deterioration.

Our forefathers took great pride and comfort in canning and pickling, and today, so can we. It's far more satisfying to open a jar of home-canned peaches or sweet gherkins than one of the mass-produced products one buys

at the supermarket. There's a sense of pride in giving a gift of homemade rhubarb ginger jam or in saying to a friend, "Won't you try my homemade peach chutney?" For many, there is a nostalgic pleasure in recreating spicy relishes and sparkling jellies remembered from childhood. And for others, canning and pickling are delicious new culinary fields to explore.

And explore we will. This book is a comprehensive guide to canning and pickling all kinds of food using the best up-to-date methods and recipes available. Both the experienced cook and the beginner will find this book an invaluable reference during the canning and pickling season.

The following four chapters cover recipes and processes for canning: jellies, jams, and other fruit preserves; fruits, tomatoes, and fruit juices; and vegetables, meats, and poultry. The sixth chapter, "All About Pickling," provides a detailed guide for making all kinds of pickles, including those by the time-honored process of fermentation. Chapter 7, "Specialties of the House," will be of interest to canners and picklers alike; it features a fine collection of distinctive recipes for everything from pickled herbs to berry syrup.

Put up bushels of apples as chutneys, butters, conserves, or pie filling.

The antique canning equipment shown here dates back to the 1800s when canning was invented.

Each chapter presents a detailed step-by-step method for preparing, packing, and processing canned or pickled foods. Color photographs accompany the explanations to take the guesswork out of the procedures. Following each section, a Problem Solver chart describes common problems that may occur and tells you how to avoid them.

Preserving seasonal foods for a day when they will not be available fresh is not only smart, it's economical. If green beans are a favorite of yours, you can save up to half of what you'd spend for them in the winter by home-canning beans when they're plentiful, inexpensive, and at their best.

Today, vast new growing areas worldwide, jet-age shipping, improved refrigeration and storage, and greenhouse growing make many fresh foods available the year around. Yet, foods preserved at home during the peak of their season often are more

flavorful than commercially sold foods, which may be picked before they're ripe and then shipped thousands of miles to be packaged and sold. When you can your own foods, you have control over the quality of what goes into the jar. Also, you have the freedom to add your own personal touch to the recipe.

How to Select, Harvest, and Purchase Foods for Canning

For the best home-canned goods, it's essential to use the freshest, most flavorful produce obtainable. The more flavor the produce has, the more flavor it will retain after it has been canned and stored for the winter.

As soon as fruits and vegetables are harvested, their quality begins to deteriorate. Chemical processes that occur during growth continue after harvesting and cause a rapid loss of moisture and flavor. On warm days, a

noticeable loss of sweetness can be detected only a few minutes after harvesting vegetables such as peas, asparagus, and sweet corn.

Select produce that is fully ripe—preferably vine, bush, or tree ripened—and firm. Underripe produce, although firm, is not as flavorful or sweet as mature produce. Examine each fruit or vegetable carefully. Choose only those that are fresh, firm, and free of bruised spots, blemishes, or any indications of spoilage. If you purchase produce in lugs or boxes, remember to check the quality of the produce at the bottom of the container. Don't be misled by a perfect-looking top layer.

If you harvest your own produce, pick it in the morning when it is still cool; it will stay fresh and flavorful longer. Place the picked fruits or vegetables in containers made of cloth, wood, or loosely woven materials, rather than in plastic bags or

metal containers. An open container permits air to circulate and heat to dissipate. Your produce will retain its fresh quality longest if cooled immediately after it is harvested or purchased.

For the best flavor and texture in your canned goods, it's also essential to process fresh produce as soon as possible after it's harvested. If you cannot prepare and process it at once, refrigerate the foods immediately after harvesting and until they are used.

It's not necessary to have a garden or orchard in your backyard to obtain fruits and vegetables suitable for preserving. There are many ways for urban dwellers and nongardeners to obtain really fresh produce.

One of the best ways is to shop the countryside at U-pick farms and farms that sell directly to the public. Many states and counties publish farm trail maps listing farmers

U-pick orchards are inexpensive sources of good produce.

who sell produce from their farms. You can also check the want ads in your local newspaper. Or, write to the Chamber of Commerce in nearby small towns and ask where fresh produce is available for picking or purchase. Not only will you save money, but the freshness, flavor, and texture of the produce will be much better than that of produce found in stores. Take a cooler with you on your produce-buying excursions to the country. Pack a picnic in it to enjoy along the way, and later fill it with the produce you buy, to keep it cool and fresh during the trip home.

You can also purchase freshly harvested fruits and vegetables from farmers who bring their produce into urban areas and set up farmers' markets. Watch for produce trucks parked along highways, too.

Food co-ops often carry very fresh, inexpensive pro-duce. If you don't belong to a co-op, ask the buyer at your local supermarket if he'll special-order an extra quantity of produce for you.

Wholesale produce terminals sometimes will sell items at wholesale prices to individuals willing to purchase in large quantities. Fruits and vegetables are sold by the bushel, the box, the crate, the peck, or the lug. How many pounds each of these containers holds depends on the shape and density of the produce in it. Take a look at the chart on page 9 to get an idea of how much a certain amount of fresh fruit will yield when canned. If a bushel of peaches is too much for you to use, get together with neighbors and friends to buy in bulk and share the lot.

The following chart is a guide to seasonal peaks when you can obtain the best quantity and quality of produce at the best price.

Harvest Seasons

Produce	JAN	FEB	MAR	APR	MAY	JUN	JUL	AUG	SEP	OCT	NOV	DEC
Apples						X	X	X	X	X	X	
Apricots						X	X	X				
Artichokes				X	X							
Asparagus				X	X	X						
Bananas	X	X	X	X	X	X	X	X	X	X	X	X
Beans							X	X	X			
Beets							X	X	X			
Blackberries						X	X	X				
Blueberries	X					X	X	X				
Broccoli	X	X	X	X	X	X	X	X	X	X	X	X
Brussels sprouts	X	X	X	X	X	X	X	X	X	X	X	X
Cabbage	X	X	X	X	X	X	X	X	X	X	X	X
Carrots	X	X	X	X	X	X	X	X	X	X	X	X
Cauliflower	X	X	X	X	X	X	X	X	X	X	X	X
Celery	X	X	X	X	X	X	X	X	X	X	X	X
Cherries					X	X	X					
Corn						X	X	X	X			
Cranberries									X	X	X	
Cucumbers					X	X	X	X				
Currants						X	X	X				
Eggplant							X	X	X			
Figs						X	X	X	X	X		
Garlic	X	X	X	X	X	X	X	X	X	X	X	X
Grapefruit	X	X	X	X	X					X	X	X
Grapes							X	X	X	X	X	
Horseradish	X	X	X	X	X	X	X	X	X	X	X	X
Lemons	X	X	X	X	X	X	X	X	X	X	X	X
Limes						X	X	X				
Mangoes					X	X	X	X				
Mushrooms	X	X	X	X	X	X	X	X	X	X	X	X
Muskmelons						X	X	X	X			
Nectarines						X	X	X	X			
Okra						X	X	X	X	X		
Onions	X	X	X	X	X	X	X	X	X	X	X	X
Oranges	X	X	X	X	X	X	X	X	X	X	X	X
Papayas						X	X	X	X			
Parsnips	X	X	X	X	X	X	X	X	X	X	X	X
Peaches						X	X	X	X			
Pears							X	X	X	X	X	
Peppers							X	X	X	X		
Persimmons										X	X	X
Pineapple			X	X	X	X						
Plums						X	X	X	X			
Raspberries						X	X	X	X	X		
Rhubarb				X	X	X						
Rutabagas	X	X	X	X	X	X	X	X	X	X	X	X
Spinach			X	X	X	X	X	X	X	X		
Strawberries				X	X	X						
Tangerines	X										X	X
Tomatoes						X	X	X	X			
Turnips	X	X	X	X	X	X	X	X	X	X	X	X
Watermelon						X	X	X	X			
Zucchini						X	X	X	X	X		

Planning a Garden for Preserving

For those with a garden or fruit trees in the backyard, canning and pickling become natural activities associated with the harvest season. With a little forethought, you can plant a garden especially suited for preserving, which will optimize your output and enjoyment of the task. The well-planned garden will yield just enough fruits and vegetables to eat fresh in season and the right amount, at the right time, to preserve.

Planning begins in the winter with the arrival of seed catalogs. Read through them carefully. As you select your seeds, have handy a list of the items you would like to preserve. Many hybrids have been developed just for canning and pickling. For those items you would also like to eat fresh, choose two var-

ieties, one for eating and one for canning. Note the time required for the plant to mature.

You can further increase your enjoyment of preserving by planting with the seasonal progression of vegetables and fruits in mind. Plan your garden so that you will not be faced with bushels of produce all ready to be canned at the same time. Stagger plantings to prevent bottlenecks and to maximize yields. Successive plantings may be made all summer, as long as the last planting matures before the first frost. Also, you can plan your planting schedule so that complementary produce will mature at the same time. For example, to make dill pickles, you'll want the dill to mature about the same time the pickling cucumbers ripen.

Seeds, such as those for pickling cucumbers, were developed just for canning. Above: Plan your garden so that produce ripens in succession.

Fresh Produce Yields

Produce	Weight	Quantity	Yield
Almonds	3½ pounds	100 unshelled	4½ cups
Apples	1 pound 48–50 pounds	6 medium 1 bushel	3 cups chopped 20 quarts chopped
Apricots	1 pound	8–14 medium	3 cups whole 2 cups halved
Bananas	1 pound	3 medium	1¼ cups mashed 2–2½ cups sliced
Beans, green	1 pound	3–4 cups	2⅔–3⅔ cups, snapped or cut
Beets	1 pound	4–6 medium	3½ cups cooked, diced
Broccoli	1½–2½ pounds	1 bunch	4–4½ cups chopped
Brussels sprouts	1 pound	15–20 sprouts	3½ cups
Cabbage	2 pounds	1 head	7–8 cups shredded 3 cups cooked
Carrots	1 pound	4 large	2½ cups sliced or diced 2 cups chopped, cooked
Cauliflower	1½ pounds	1 head	4 cups flowerets
Celery	1 pound	8–12 stalks	4 cups diced
Cherries	1 pound	3 cups	2½ cups pitted
Corn	12–18 pounds	16–20 ears	2 quarts cut
Cranberries	1 pound	4–6 cups	2–2½ cups ground
Cucumbers	1 pound 6 pounds 6 pounds 9–12 pounds	2 large 100 very small 50 medium 50 3- to 4-inch	2 cups sliced 1 gallon whole 1 gallon whole 6–8 quarts whole
Currants	1 pound	2⅔ cups	2–2½ cups
Figs	1 pound	12–18 medium	2½–3 cups chopped
Gooseberries	1 pound	2⅔ cups	2⅔ cups
Grapefruit	1¼ pounds	1 large	1¾ cups broken 10–12 sections
Grapes	1 pound	2⅔ cups	2 cups halved 1 cup purée
Lemons	4 pounds	12 large	2½ cups juice 12 teaspoons grated peel
Lima beans	1 pound	100 pods	2–3 cups shelled
Limes	2¾ pounds	12 medium	1½–2 cups juice
Mangoes	1 pound	2–4	2 cups peeled, sliced
Mushrooms	1 pound	2½ cups	1½ cups sliced
Muskmelons	2 pounds	1 medium	1 cup chopped
Nectarines	1 pound	3–5 medium	2 cups peeled, sliced
Olives	1 pound	135 "small" 70 "mammoth" 40 "colossal" 32 "super colossal"	Same Same Same Same
Onions	1 pound	3 large or 4–4½ medium	2–2½ cups diced 2 cups chopped or ground
Oranges	6 pounds	12 medium	3–5 cups juice 6 cups diced
Peaches	1 pound 48 pounds	3–5 medium 1 bushel	2–2½ cups peeled, sliced 18–24 quarts, peeled
Pears	1 pound 48–50 pounds	4–5 medium 1 bushel	2⅔ cups peeled, sliced 20–25 quarts
Pecans	2½ pounds	75 unshelled	3 cups, halved
Peppers	1 pound	4 large	2 cups trimmed or chopped
Pineapple	3 pounds	1 medium	3–3½ cups peeled, diced
Plums	1 pound 50–56 pounds	12–20 medium 1 bushel	2 cups sliced 24–30 quarts
Prunes (dried)	1 pound	30–40 medium	4 cups cooked 2½ cups cooked, chopped
Raisins (seedless)	1 pound	3 cups	2½ cups chopped
Raisins (seeded)	1 pound	2½ cups	2 cups chopped
Squash (summer)	2¼ pounds	12 medium	6 cups ground
Strawberries	1 quart	3 cups	1 pint crushed 1¼ cups purée
Tomatoes	1 pound 8 pounds 53 pounds	4 medium 32 medium 1 bushel	3 cups sliced 4 quarts peeled, sliced 15–20 quarts
Turnips	1 pound	3–4 medium	3½–4½ cups sliced
Walnuts (English)	2½ pounds	50 unshelled	4 cups halved
Watermelon	30 pounds	10 pounds rind	3¼–4 quarts chopped
Zucchini	1 pound	3 medium	2¼ cups sliced

Fresh Produce Yields for Canning

In the adjacent chart you will find an extensive list of fresh produce yields. Use it as a guide for determining how much of an item you should grow, harvest, or purchase to meet your canning needs.

Top: Ripe blackcap raspberries are ready to pick and turn into luscious preserves in summer.
Above: Peaches reach the peak of their season in late summer.

Guide to Preserving Produce

Produce	Jellies	Jams	Preserves	Conserves	Marmalades	Butters	Canning	Relishes	Chutneys	Pickles	Juice
Apples	●			●		●	●	●	●	●	●
Apricots	●	●	●	●		●	●		●	●	●
Bananas		●							●	●	
Beans, green							●			●	
Beets	●						●	●		●	
Broccoli										●	
Brussels sprouts										●	
Cabbage								●		●	
Carrots							●	●		●	●
Cauliflower								●		●	
Celery							●	●		●	
Cherries	●	●	●	●			●		●	●	●
Corn							●	●		●	
Cranberries	●	●	●	●			●	●	●		●
Cucumbers								●		●	
Currants	●	●	●	●							
Figs		●	●	●			●		●	●	
Gooseberries	●	●	●	●			●			●	
Grapefruit					●						●
Grapes	●	●	●	●		●	●			●	●
Lemons	●			●	●				●	●	●
Lima Beans							●				
Limes				●	●				●		●
Mangoes									●	●	
Mushrooms							●			●	
Melons									●	●	
Nectarines		●		●		●	●		●	●	●
Onions							●			●	
Oranges					●						●
Peaches		●	●	●		●	●		●	●	●
Pears		●		●		●	●	●	●	●	●
Peppers	●						●	●	●	●	
Pineapple		●		●			●		●	●	●
Plums	●	●		●		●	●		●	●	●
Prunes	●	●	●	●		●	●		●	●	●
Raspberries	●	●	●				●				●
Strawberries	●	●	●								●
Squash, summer							●	●		●	
Squash, winter							●		●	●	
Tomatoes		●					●	●	●	●	●
Watermelon										●	

Preserving Possibilities

No matter how well you plan your garden or how carefully you estimate your needs, more often than not in the midst of the harvest season, you will be faced with a surplus of ripe vegetables and fruits and a lack of ideas about how to use them. The preceding chart lists all kinds of fresh produce and the many different ways each can be preserved. So the next time your tomato vines are full of ripe, red fruits, don't just can them; make relishes, chutneys, pickles, and juice, too.

Resources and Reading

If you have a question or problem or want more information about canning and pickling, there are many sources to which you can turn.

Bulletins on home canning and pickling are available from your county or state cooperative extension service. Agents at the extension service offices have a wealth of knowledge and information about canning and are happy to answer questions and offer advice. Extension offices are located at land-grant universities. Look in the telephone directory under Extension Service, or in the county government listings.

Government agencies publish bulletins on all facets of home preserving. Write to the Superintendent of Documents, U.S. Government Printing Office, Washington, D.C. 20402 for a catalog of bulletins published by the U.S. Department of Agriculture. For additional information, write to Consumer Product Information, Public Documents Distribution Center, Pueblo, Colorado 81009. In Canada, write to your local provincial agriculture department or to the Canada Department of Agriculture, Information Division, Sir John Carling Building, 930 Carling Avenue, Ottawa, Ontario K1A 0C7.

Home economists at the major jar manufacturing companies will answer consumer questions and handle problems and complaints. Write to the consumer service departments at the Ball Corporation, Muncie, Indiana 47302 and Kerr Glass Manufacturing Corporation, Sand Springs, Oklahoma 74063.

Additional Reading

Ball Blue Book: Ball Corporation, Muncie, Indiana.

Better than Store-Bought: Helen Witty and Elizabeth Schneider Colchie, Harper & Row, Publishers, New York, 1979.

Fine Preserving: Catherine Plagemann, Simon and Schuster, New York, 1967.

Home Canning and Freezing: Jacqueline Heriteau, Grosset & Dunlap, New York, 1975.

Introduction to Cooking with the Amana Radarange Cookbook: Amana Refrigeration, Inc., Amana, Iowa, 1980.

Kerr Home Canning and Freezing Book: Kerr Glass Manufacturing Corporation, Sand Springs, Oklahoma.

The Microwave Guide and Cookbook: General Electric Company, 1977.

Putting Food By: Ruth Hertzberg, Beatrice Vaughan, and Janet Greene, The Stephen Greene Press, Brattleboro, Vermont, 1975.

The U.S. Department of Agriculture has published these helpful pamphlets (the address to write for them is on page 10):

Canning, Freezing, and Storing Garden Produce: USDA Information Bulletin No. 410.

Home Canning Fruits and Vegetables: USDA Home and Garden Bulletin No. 8.

Home Canning of Meat and Poultry: USDA Home and Garden Bulletin No. 106.

How to Make Jellies, Jams, and Preserves at Home: USDA Home and Garden Bulletin No. 56.

Making Pickles and Relishes at Home: USDA Home and Garden Bulletin No. 92.

Pressure Canners, Use and Care: USDA Home and Garden Bulletin No. 30.

Resources for Equipment and Cookware

Canning and pickling don't require much in the way of specialized equipment, and you're likely to find just about everything you'll need at local hardware and department stores. Most supermarkets carry an assortment of containers and lids. Restaurant supply houses stock big crocks, steam pressure canners, and other heavy or special equipment. When you've exhausted these sources, try mail order catalogs. You can order catalogs for equipment and cookware from the following sources:

Bazaar Français
666 Sixth Avenue
New York, NY 10028
(212) 243–6660

Nasco
1524 Princeton Avenue
Modesto, CA 95350
(209) 529–6957

Paprikás Weiss
1546 Second Avenue
New York, NY 10028
(212) 288–6117

Smithfield Implement Co.
97 North Main Street
Smithfield, UT 84335
(801) 563–5035

Whole Earth Access Co.
2466 Shattuck Avenue
Berkeley, CA 94704
(415) 548–8040

Whole Earth Access Co.
Ashby and 7th Street
Berkeley, CA 94710
(415) 845–3000

Why Food Spoils

Almost all food, whether plant or animal in origin, is subject to deterioration and eventual decay. If food is not properly preserved, spoilage organisms will grow, speeding its deterioration and contaminating it.

Properly canned foods are perfectly safe—grocery-store shelves are laden with them. It's only when foods are improperly canned that you run the risk of food spoilage. This complete guide to canning strives to eliminate that risk and enhance the enjoyment and safety of home canning. Remember, the keys to successful canning are careful handling and perfect sealing, along with proper processing times and temperatures. Using faulty methods or improper equipment will increase the chance of unsatisfactory results.

Food spoilage has two principal sources: active enzymes and microorganisms. Both are found naturally in plants and animals, and even in soil, water, and air.

Enzymes **in plant and animal tissues cause the tissues to mature, ripen, and eventually decay. Long after fruits and vegetables have been harvested or animals slaughtered, the enzymes within the food remain active, causing the food tissues to break down, and color and flavor to deteriorate.**

Microorganisms **are the molds, yeast, and bacteria present in all fresh foods. Active microscopic fungi known as** *molds* **develop as fine threads on food. Some molds are cultivated deliberately, but most molds produce unpleasant flavors and may even be poisonous. In addition, molds eat the natural acid present in foods. Acid is necessary to inhibit the growth of contaminating bacteria in foods. Low acid levels in foods allow these harmful organisms to develop.**

Another microorganism found in foods is *yeast.* **In most canned goods this substance will encourage fats and starches to oxidize and turn rancid. As with molds, severe cold inactivates yeast, moderate temperatures encourage its growth, and temperatures above 140°F kill it.**

Bacteria **are microorganisms more difficult to destroy than molds and yeast. For example, the bacterium** *Salmonella* **is killed at temperatures above 140°F, but** *Staphylococcus aureas* **produces a toxin that is destroyed only by many hours of boiling, or at temperatures much higher than boiling.**

Clostridium botulinum **is an extremely dangerous bacterium that produces botulism. While rare, botulism is usually fatal.** *Clostridium botulinum* **is commonly found in water and soil. It is harmless in the presence of oxygen; however, in an anaerobic (airless) environment, such as a sealed jar, the bacterium produces spores that multiply and produce poisonous toxins. The spores are destroyed when low-acid vegetables, meats, and poultry are processed in a steam pressure canner under 10 pounds of pressure (240°F) for altitudes up to 2,000 feet. (See page 55.) Fruits and pickles can be processed safely in a boiling-water bath because their high acidity inhibits the formation of these toxins.**

Detection of spoilage is outlined on page 55 in Chapter 5, as well as in the Problem Solver charts that accompany each section. Your local health department can also help you identify spoilage.

A Short Course On Canning

The "how-to" of canning from a guide for using canning equipment, to a thorough description of how to pack, process, and seal canned goods. This will be your basic reference for canning all sorts of foods correctly.

There's no mystery to canning. Like many projects, it may appear difficult at first, but once you get the hang of it, you'll wonder why you didn't try it before. If you've never done any canning, it's easier to share the first experience with a friend, relative, or neighbor. Not only can you share in the expense of equipment and food, but an extra pair of hands will be a great help the first time you run through the procedure.

Actually, the term *canning* is something of a misnomer. At home, foods are "put up" in jars more often than in cans. The canning process is simple: Food is packed into jars and the jars are capped and then heated. Sustained high heat inactivates the enzymes and kills microorganisms that cause food spoilage.

This chapter will familiarize you with the essentials of canning. It includes everything from how to pack and seal a jar to how to operate a steam pressure canner. After reading it, you should be able to can everything from a

A jar of baby carrots is lifted from a steam pressure canner after being processed for 30 minutes.

delicate strawberry jelly to a robust chili con carne. Not only will this chapter act as a reference for the next three, but it will prepare you for putting up pickles as well; read it carefully before you begin any canning or pickling project.

Tooling Up

You probably own most of the equipment needed for canning. Any equipment you don't have can be purchased at hardware and department stores and at many supermarkets. Refer to the list of equipment sources on pp. 11 if you can't find what you need in local stores.

Jars

The jar is the common denominator in home canning. The most common type of jar made specially for home canning is the Mason jar (see illustration, page 14), which has a self-sealing lid that is held in place by a metal ring band. In the mid-1800s, an American, John Mason, developed a canning jar that sealed itself during the heating process. The canning jars we use today are modern versions of Mason's invention, and commonly bear his name. Companies that produce Mason jars include the Ball Corporation, Kerr Glass Manufacturing Corporation,

and the Dominion Glass Company Limited in Canada. Jars are available in half-pint, pint, and quart sizes with narrow or wide mouths. Half-pint and pint jars are the best choices for jelly, jam, and other fruit preserves; pint and quart jars are suitable for packing whole tomatoes, fruits and vegetables, and large pieces of food. You can reuse jars (but not the self-sealing lids) as long as they are free of nicks and cracks.

Canning utensils include spoons, brushes, and peelers.

Jar caps consisting of flat metal lids with sealing compound and metal ring bands come with new Mason jars; they're also sold separately. Lids can be used only once; however, the ring bands may be reused if they're not rusted or bent. Store unused lids, ring bands, and jars in a cool, dry place.

To use a Mason jar, fill the jar and wipe the rim and screw threads with a damp cloth. Place the lid on the jar with the sealing compound next to the glass and screw on the metal ring band firmly, but not too tightly.

The step-by-step instructions in this book assume the use of Mason jars. If using another type of jar, follow the directions below for filling and sealing. One type of jar has a hinged glass lid that is clamped in place over a rubber ring to ensure a tight seal. (See illustration, page 14.) These jars are mostly used for canning fruits, fruit preserves, and pickles.

To use clamp-type jars, cover the rubber rings with simmering, not boiling, water. After several minutes, fit the rings onto the rims of each lid. Fill the jars and clamp the lids shut. Process the jars in a boiling-water bath according to directions. After processing, cool the

jars to room temperature in the water. Then, remove the jars from the canner and let them cool 12 hours more.

Test the seal by gently unlocking the clamp of each cooled jar. Holding the jar by the lid, lift it very slightly. If the jar remains closed, it has sealed properly and may be reclamped and stored. Jars that do not seal need to be reprocessed with a new rubber ring, or you may refrigerate the jar and eat the contents within a few days.

Old-fashioned canning jars, sometimes called "lightening jars," have domed glass lids that clamp down over rubber rings. (See illustration.) These jars may be used safely if they're made of tempered glass and have double, not single, wire clamps. Lightening jars have two drawbacks: The rubber rings are not reuseable and replacement rings may be difficult to find; and once the jars have been processed, it's hard to determine if they are sealed. Lightening jars, like the jars with hinged lids, can be used only if foods will be processed in a boiling-water bath. Do not use them for foods that must be processed in a steam pressure canner.

To use a lightening jar, fit a wet rubber ring to the sealing ledge on the neck of a filled jar. Put on the glass lid so that it rests on the rubber ring. Grasp the longest of the two wire clamps, pulling it up to the small groove in the lid. Let the shorter wire hang down while the food is being processed. After processing, immediately clamp down the shorter wire to seal the jar.

Another old-fashioned type of jar, which is still made but not widely available, has a porcelain-lined zinc cap and a rubber ring. (See illustration.) The caps can be reused if they're in good condition, but the rings must not be. To use the jar, fit a new rubber ring to the sealing ledge of an empty jar. Pack the jar, wipe the ring

and jar lip clean, and screw the cap on firmly. Then unscrew it 1/4 inch—to allow the air in the jar to vent properly. Immediately after processing, screw the cap down tightly to complete the seal. Once the jar has cooled, tilt it to see if it leaks. Jars that leak have not sealed.

Fancy jars with brightly colored lids and quilted jelly glasses can be purchased just for jelly-making. When you seal jelly with paraffin, you can use many sizes and shapes of jars and glasses, as long as they can withstand the boiling temperature needed to sterilize them.

Do not can foods in jars you've saved from mayonnaise, pickles, peanut butter, and the like. They will not seal properly and may not take the heat required in canning.

Utensils

Many of the utensils you will need are standard in today's kitchen: measuring utensils, a ladle, sharp knives, long-handled spoons, a colander, a minute timer, and a cooling rack or towel. A vegetable brush to clean produce, a skimmer or metal spoon to remove scum from jelly mixtures, a wide-mouth funnel to fill jars, a jar lifter to lift hot jars out of boiling water, a kitchen scale, and heavy rubber gloves come in handy. A jelly bag and stand are helpful for straining fruit juice for jelly-making; however, several thicknesses of closely woven cheesecloth or firm, unbleached muslin set inside a colander may be substituted. Some canning processes may require more specialized tools, such as a

Pictured above are many different types and sizes of canning jars and lids. The Mason jars in the center are most commonly used. The large, clamp-type jars in the background are suitable for canning fruits, preserves, and pickles.

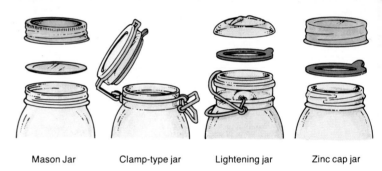

Mason Jar   Clamp-type jar   Lightening jar   Zinc cap jar

Canning in boiling-water bath

2-inch

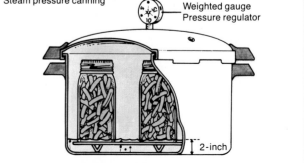

Steam pressure canning

Weighted gauge
Pressure regulator

2-inch

candy or jelly thermometer for testing the jell point of fruit preserves, or a food mill for puréeing fruits into creamy butters.

Also, you will need a 6-quart or larger pot in which to prepare food and a saucepan in which to scald jar lids and rings. Nonreactive pots of heavy enameled metal or stainless steel are best. Do not use zinc (galvanized), aluminum, or cast iron pots, since they may react chemically with the acids and salts in foods, producing unpleasant colors and metallic flavors.

Canners

For heat-processing fruit preserves and high-acid fresh fruits, tomatoes, and juices, a *water-bath canner* is indispensable. However, any large, covered kettle that is deep enough to allow the jar tops to be covered with an inch or two of hot water and still allow extra space for boiling may be substituted. Canners are fitted with a divided wire rack or basket that keeps jars from touching each other and from resting on the bottom or against the sides of the canner during processing. A round cake rack elevated at least 3/4 inch off the bottom of the kettle can serve this purpose when improvising.

Most water-bath canners on the market come fitted with a wire basket. Wire baskets work well for processing pint or quart jars, but they're frustrating when canning half-pints because the small jars slip through the wires and end up on the bottom of the canner. When you can fruit preserves or relishes in small jars, you'll have to improvise—try a round cake rack, or if you have a steam pressure canner, use the rack from it.

A *steam pressure canner* is essential for canning low-acid foods such as vegetables, meats, and poultry. (Do not confuse a steam pressure canner with a pres-

sure cooker or pressure saucepan—they are not the same.) Quite different from a water-bath canner, the steam pressure canner is a heavy kettle, usually made of cast aluminum, with a cover that can be locked down to make it steam-tight. The cover is fitted with a pressure gauge, a petcock or pressure regulator to let steam exhaust before processing begins, and a safety valve that blows when the pressure inside the canner becomes too great.

There are two types of pressure canners on the market—one has a weighted gauge; the other, a dial. The weighted gauge is simple, accurate, and never needs calibrating. It automatically limits pressure to a preset level of 5, 10, or 15 pounds. The dial gauge has a needle that indicates pressure on a numbered instrument.

Steam pressure canners are available in various sizes; 16-quart and 22-quart sizes are common. These canners are expensive, but last for years when you keep their sealing rims and parts clean and in good working order.

Canning equipment (clockwise from top): steam pressure canner, jelly bag and stand, large measuring cup, scale, colander, jar lifter, long-handled spoons, vegetable brush, ladles, thermometer, cooling rack, labels, cheesecloth, knives, measuring cups, timer, food mill, water-bath canning rack and jars, wide mouth funnel, and water-bath canner.

Getting Organized

Good planning is the secret to successful canning. Take a moment to list the kinds of canned comestibles you'll want to put away for the months to come. Examine your supply of jars, lids, caps, and rubber rings. Check jars for any nicks, cracks, and sharp edges that might prevent a good seal. An imperfection in a jar's sealing capability could admit air, ruining the contents. Discard dry or cracked rubber rings, and dented or rusted ring bands and lids. Check your other equipment to be sure it's in perfect working condition.

Don't wait until the last minute to buy jars and extra fittings. It's discouraging to be faced with a bushel of peaches rotting on the back porch because the stores have run out of canning lids.

Preserving the goodness of fresh food begins with the raw product. Harvest or purchase firm yet ripe fruits and young, tender vegetables at their peak of flavor and maturity. See Chapter 1 for more information about where to find the best produce and all the different ways each type can be preserved. Wash and prepare produce and other food as directed in the charts and recipes that follow in each chapter. Prepare only as much food as can be processed in one canner load at a time. While the first batch is processing, prepare the next batch and have it ready for the canner as soon as the first batch is finished.

You'll enjoy canning more and probably do a better job if you spread your canning sessions over a series of days, rather than spending an entire day in the kitchen processing load after load and filling jar after jar. For best results, always set aside enough time so you won't be rushed and forced to cut corners in the procedures. Use only small quantities of food, and work quickly and efficiently as you pack and seal the jars. Fresh food, particularly produce, loses its flavor and texture rapidly after harvesting. Once the food is sealed and stored, preservation begins and deterioration slows considerably.

Scald lids to soften their sealing compound.

Packing the Jars

Fruits, vegetables, and meats can be either raw-packed or hot-packed into jars. These methods are explained in detail in Chapters 4 and 5. In the charts and recipes throughout this book, directions are given for both methods unless a particular food is best packed only one way.

Jars must be clean and hot when they're filled. Scald lids before they're used, following the manufacturer's directions. Do not boil them, since this can ruin the lid's sealing compound. Only jars used for jellies (or for any other items that are not heat-processed) need to be sterilized. Boil them for 15 minutes to sterilize.

Many canning books recommend that jars be left in hot water until they're ready to be used so they won't crack when filled with boiling-hot food. You may find it more convenient to take the jars from the sink or dishwasher, set them upright in the oven on the oven rack, and then turn the oven on to 200°F. This method keeps them dry as well as hot. Remove the jars from the oven and fill them one at a time.

Handle hot jars with heavy rubber gloves. The gloves will help you maintain a firm grip on the jars, and they'll protect your hands from heat and spills as you put food and hot liquids into jars.

As you pack jars, you must leave some *headspace*—the space between the jar's lid and its contents. Headspace allows for the expansion of food while it's being processed. Insufficient headspace will cause the seal to break and the jar's contents to seep out. Too much headspace may cause food at the top of the jar to discolor and possibly cause the jar's contents to spoil. The charts and recipes throughout this book specify the correct amount of headspace.

Processing the Food

There are two basic methods of heat-processing food—the *boiling-water bath method* and the *steam pressure method*. Jams and fruit preserves, fruits, tomatoes, and fruit juices are safely canned by the boiling-water bath method. Vegetables, meats, and poultry require higher processing temperatures and must be canned by the steam pressure method. With either method, process only one type of food and one size jar at a time.

You may have heard the term *open-kettle canning*. Dating back to the early 1800s, this was the first canning process used. In open-kettle canning, boiling hot, fully cooked food is packed into hot, sterilized jars; the

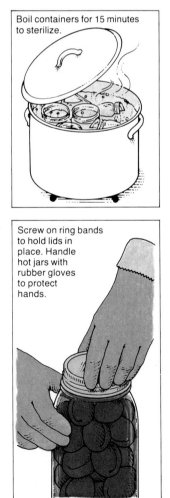

Boil containers for 15 minutes to sterilize.

Screw on ring bands to hold lids in place. Handle hot jars with rubber gloves to protect hands.

jars are not heat-processed. Today, canning experts agree that this method is safe only for making jelly.

An unacceptable way to process foods is in the oven. Dry heat does not penetrate the center of the jar adequately, and in fact, jars may explode if they're exposed to high oven temperatures.

Sealing the Jars

The canning job is not done until you're sure the jars have sealed. The mechanism of sealing is simple. During heat-processing, the contents of the jars expand and some air is forced out of the jars. When the jars cool, the remaining air contracts, creating a partial vacuum that pulls the lids tightly against the jar rims and holds them in place. The vacuum and the lid's sealing compound maintain the seal. As the jars cool, you may hear a loud popping noise. This is an indication that a jar has just sealed. Sealing is not always accompanied by a loud noise, however. To test for a seal, press the center of the lid of a completely cooled jar with your finger. If the lid stays down, the jar is sealed.

Once the jars have sealed, the flat lids will adhere to the jar rims, so you may remove and reuse the ring bands. To loosen a band that sticks, cover it with a hot, damp cloth for several minutes, then unscrew. Never tighten ring bands after processing —doing so could loosen the lid's sealing compound and let air into the jar.

If a jar fails to seal, refrigerate and eat the contents within a short period. If many jars fail to seal, a problem may have occurred during processing. Check the appropriate Problem Solver chart. Food may be recanned and reprocessed, but we do not recommend it because much of the food value, flavor, and color will be lost.

Labeling and Storing Canned Goods

Even though home-canned foods are visible through glass, it's amazing how easily we forget which recipe we followed or when the food was canned. To avoid aggravation later on, write the name of the product and the date it was canned on the lid of each jar with a marking pen, or attach a label. Also, keep a record in a notebook —the item canned, the recipe followed, the date, and the number of jars canned— and check off the items as you use them. The following year, this record will help you determine what, how much, and when to preserve.

Canned foods stored in a cool (below 70°F), dark, dry place will retain their flavor, color, and nutritional value for about a year. As the year progresses, the flavor, color, and food value decrease, so try to eat the earliest dated canned goods before more recently canned items. Warm storage temperatures and light will hasten discoloration and flavor changes. Once opened, canned foods need to be refrigerated.

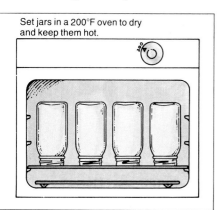
Set jars in a 200°F oven to dry and keep them hot.

Fill jars

Headspace

Lift jars straight up to avoid tipping contents

Test for a seal by pressing lid of cooled jar.

Label canned foods with the name of the recipe and date you canned it. Use rubber stamps and cloth for a decorative touch.

Jellies, Jams, and Other Fruit Preserves

Herein lie the secrets of success for making delectable homemade jellies, jams and fruit preserves. In addition to many time-tested, mouth-watering recipes, you'll find precise step-by-step guides for making them right.

It's immensely satisfying to see a pantry shelf laden with jars of shimmering jellies and thick, homemade jams. There's nothing better than piping hot biscuits or thick slices of toasted bread slathered with these homemade delicacies—especially first thing in the morning.

Fruit preserves are even popular with people who do very little canning because they are so easy to make and usually are enjoyed by all. In a few short hours you can turn just-picked fruit into blue-ribbon specialties.

Many different types of fruit preserves can be made by cooking fruit with sugar. These include jellies, jams, marmalades, conserves, butters, and one simply called preserves.

Jellies are made from fruit juices boiled with sugar until they reach the jell point. Fine jellies are clear and shimmering. When cut, they hold their shape. Soft jellies simmered with slivers of citrus peel fall into the category of *marmalades*. *Jams* are made

What tastes better than a piece of bread spread with jelly, jam, or preserves? Here, raspberry jam (recipe, page 35) whets our appetites.

from crushed or chopped fruit cooked to a thick, spreadable consistency. *Conserves* are a marriage of two or more fruits and often include nuts and raisins. *Preserves* contain whole fruit or large chunks suspended in a brilliant, heavy syrup. *Butters* are fruit purées reduced to a thick, spreadable consistency.

Equipment Needs

The equipment you'll need to make these homemade fruit preserves includes a deep, flat-bottomed pot roomy enough to boil jelly and jam rapidly without spillovers. Jelly that boils over onto the stove is no fun to clean up! For heat-processing jars, use a water-bath canner or a large, covered kettle deep enough so that the jars can be completely submerged in the water, with space above for the water to boil. Measuring cups, sharp knives, a long-handled spoon, a ladle, and a timer are standard utensils. A food mill, jar lifter, wide-mouth funnel, and candy or jelly thermometer are optional, but certainly handy to have. To strain juices for jellies, a jelly bag and stand are useful; however, several thicknesses of closely woven cheesecloth or unbleached muslin set

inside a colander suspended over a deep bowl may be substituted.

Unless you plan to refrigerate and use preserves within a few weeks, they should be put up in jars. Standard half-pint and pint canning jars are the best choices for jams and other preserves. Fancy jars with brightly covered lids and quilted jelly glasses will enhance the appearance of your jellies and

Fresh, red-ripe raspberries are at their peak in the summer.

make nice containers for the preserves you plan to use as gifts. When paraffin wax is used to seal jelly containers, many sizes and shapes of jars and glasses may be used, as long as they can withstand the boiling temperature needed to sterilize them.

Starting on page 13 you'll find a detailed explanation of canning equipment.

Firm-textured, fully ripe fruit imbued with sweetness and spice creates a myriad of fruit preserves.

Fruit Preserve Ingredients

Fine jellies, jams, and other preserves consist of a balance of fruit, sugar, acid, and pectin. Full-flavored fresh *fruit* is the essence of distinctive preserves. It contributes the characteristic flavor and color, and provides at least part of the sweetness, pectin, and acid needed. Select firm, fully ripe fruit that is free of blemishes and bruises. Never use overripe fruit.

Sugar contributes flavor, serves as a preserving agent, and aids in the jelling process. Both granulated beet and cane sugars can be used with success. You can substitute honey for up to half the sugar in most recipes; however, if you prefer to use honey, follow a recipe developed especially for honey, for best results. Lemon Honey Jelly on page 25 is a delicious example. Brown sugar and molasses will mask a fruit's characteristic flavor and therefore are not recommended ingredients. For the same reason, it's best to use a light, mild honey, unless you want the honey to dominate the preserve's flavor.

Acid accentuates a fruit's natural flavor and works in conjunction with pectin to set the preserves. Use the following taste test to judge the acidity of your fruit or juice, then make any necessary adjustments in the acid content.

Acid Test

Prepare a mixture of 1 teaspoon lemon juice, 3 tablespoons water, and 2 teaspoons sugar. Compare the taste of the fruit or juice to that of the acid mixture. The tartness should be about the same. To increase the tartness of the fruit or juice, add 1 tablespoon of lemon juice for each cup of fruit or juice.

Pectin, the substance that makes fruit preserves jell, is concentrated in the seeds, skin, and flesh of fruits. The amount of pectin varies from fruit to fruit. Apples, cranberries, and most citrus fruits are high in natural pectin; strawberries, peaches, and apricots are low. The amount of pectin also varies according to the age of the fruit. Underripe fruit has more pectin than overripe fruit.

Some fruits that are medium or low in pectin require the addition of commercial or homemade pectin stock to ensure that the fruit mixture will jell properly. Jams and other fruit preserves are soft and thick, rather than firm like jelly, so they often do not require the addition of pectin.

Use the following chart to check the pectin level of the fruit you wish to make into jelly. It will help you determine whether additional pectin will be needed to make the juice set.

Pectin Content of Fruits

	High	Medium	Low
Apples, tart	●		
Apples, sweet		●	
Apricots			●
Blackberries		●	
Blueberries		●	
Boysenberries		●	
Cherries, sour		●	
Cherries, sweet		●	
Citrus fruit	●		
Cranberries	●		
Currants	●		
Elderberries		●	
Figs			●
Gooseberries	●		
Grapes		●	
Loganberries		●	
Melons		●	
Nectarines			●
Ollalieberries		●	
Peaches			●
Pears		●	
Pineapple			●
Plums, sour	●		
Plums, sweet			●
Quinces	●		
Raspberries		●	
Rhubarb			●
Strawberries			●

Pectin is available in liquid and powdered form.

How to Make Jellies

Jellies are made by cooking ripe, full-flavored fruit—often with a little water—until the fruit renders its juice. The juice is strained, combined with sugar, more pectin and acid (lemon juice) are added if necessary, and then cooked until it jells.

The Importance of Pectin in Jellies

As discussed in the introduction to this chapter, you must add pectin to fruit juices low in natural pectin; otherwise, you'll have syrup rather than jelly. Supplement a fruit's natural pectin in one of three ways: combine fruits low in natural pectin with those higher in pectin; add commercial pectin; or add home-made pectin stock. (Recipe given on following page.)

Apple-Grape Jelly (page 26) is a perfect example of a blend of fruits containing varying amounts of pectin. Not only does this combination produce a successful jell —it is also a beautiful marriage of flavors and colors. Commercial pectin is available in powdered or liquid form. Either form is satisfactory and can be used with any fruit. Because adding commercial pectin is easy and eliminates uncertainty, most of the recipes in this chapter call for it.

Use each form according to package directions, or follow recipes developed for the particular product. Powdered and liquid pectin are not interchangeable.

Connoisseurs of fine jellies prefer those made with homemade pectin. When we tested plum jelly using both homemade pectin stock and commercial liquid pectin, we discovered that the jelly made from homemade pectin took considerably longer to cook to a jell (15 minutes for homemade stock versus 1 minute for commercial pectin) but required only half as much sugar, which we found quite pleasing. Jellies made with homemade pectin stock are fruitier and richer in color than those made with commercial pectin. Try Sweet Plum Jelly and Strawberry Jelly made with homemade pectin on pages 25 and 28. We think you'll be delighted with the results.

Homemade pectin stock is produced by simmering a high-pectin fruit, such as apples, with water until it renders its juice. Then cook the juice to reduce it and concentrate the pectin. The following pectin stock recipe uses apples, but homemade stock also can be made with quinces, lemons, orange pith, or cranberries. Apples and quinces will not dominate the flavor of the fruit used for jelly-making; however, lemons, oranges, and cranberries will lend their own characteristic tastes and colors to the finished preserve.

Homemade jelly is an unbeatable treat on fresh-from-the-oven corn muffins. See pages 30–31 for delicious bread recipes.

Homemade Apple Pectin Stock

Tart, slightly underripe green apples, washed and stemmed
2 cups water for each pound of apples

1. Slice unpeeled apples (including cores and seeds) into large kettle. Add water.

2. Cover and bring to a boil. Reduce heat and simmer 20 minutes. Do not overcook. Remove from heat and allow to cool slightly.

3. Pour pulp and juice through damp jelly bag or four layers of damp cheesecloth and allow to drip undisturbed into a large bowl for 4 hours or overnight.

4. Place apple juice in large pot and bring to a boil. Boil rapidly until volume is reduced by half.

5. Quickly ladle into hot, sterilized pint or half-pint jars, leaving 1/4-inch headspace; seal.

6. Process in boiling-water bath 10 minutes.

Yield: About 1 cup pectin stock per pound of apples.

Note: Using ripe apples will produce a clearer pectin stock; however, they are not quite as high in natural pectin as underripe apples.

To use pectin for jelly-making, add 2/3 cup pectin to every 4 cups of low- or medium-pectin fruit juice. Some juices that are very low in pectin may require the addition of up to 1 cup of pectin stock for every cup of low-pectin juice. Start by adding the minimum amount of pectin stock, test for pectin level (see page 24), and continue to add the homemade pectin until the juice has sufficient pectin.

You'll experience success with all of the recipes in this section if you follow the step-by-step jelly-making method given here. Refer to it as a guide—it will take the uncertainty out of jelly-making and will help you through any rough spots. And before you dive in, reread Chapter 2 and the introduction to this chapter. Also take a look at the Problem Solver chart on page 41. We've said it before, "An ounce of prevention . . . ."

Rescuing Syrupy Jellies

Sometimes jelly made without additional pectin simply doesn't jell. If this happens, don't give up—you can often rescue syrupy jelly. Or you can turn a syrupy failure into a success by using it as a topping for ice cream or waffles, or as the base for milkshakes.

Soft jelly may result from too little sugar, pectin, or acid or from undercooking the juice mixture. To remedy the situation, you can recook the jelly with the aid of a little powdered pectin. First, measure the jelly to be recooked. For each quart of jelly, measure 1/4 cup water, 4 teaspoons powdered pectin, and 1/4 cup sugar. In a deep pot, mix the powdered pectin and water, and then bring it to a boil, stirring constantly. Add the soft jelly and bring the mixture to a full, rolling boil over high heat, stirring constantly. Boil rapidly for 30 seconds. Remove the cooked jelly from the heat, skim the top, pour it into hot, sterilized containers, and seal. Refer to the Problem Solver chart on page 41 for ways to prevent other possible jelly-making problems.

Step-by-Step Method for Making Jelly

1. *Prepare the jars or jelly glasses.* Wash and rinse containers and closures. Immerse the containers in a pan of water, bring to a boil, and boil for 15 minutes to sterilize. Allow the containers to remain in hot water or place in a low (200°F) oven until you are ready to use them. (Some dishwashers have a sterilizing cycle, which may be used to sterilize jars. Leave them in the dishwasher until needed.) Scald the lids and rings following the manufacturer's directions. Lids and rings are unnecessary when you plan to put up jelly in glasses sealed with paraffin. When you seal with paraffin, select a flared jar so that the wax can be removed easily.

2. *Prepare the fruit.* Wash fruit; remove stems and any bruised parts. Do not core or peel fruit; skin and seeds contain needed pectin. Cut large and medium-size fruit into small pieces. Crush small, soft fruit, such as berries, to start the juice flowing.

3. *Cook the fruit to extract juice.* Put crushed or chopped fruit into a deep pot. When preparing firm fruits, such as apples, add 1 cup of water to each pound of fruit. To semi-firm fruits, such as plums, add 1/4 cup of water to each pound of fruit. Soft fruits, such as berries, usually don't require additional water. For richest flavor, cook the fruit with a minimum amount of water—only enough to prevent sticking and scorching. **(Photo A.)**

　　Bring the fruit to a boil, reduce the heat, cover, and cook until tender—5 to 10 minutes for soft fruit; 15 to 20 minutes for firm fruit. Do not overcook; too much boiling reduces jelling ability and evaporates the juice. (You'll end up with fruit sauce instead of juice.)

4. *Strain the juice.* Suspend a damp jelly bag in its frame over a large bowl or line a colander with four thicknesses of damp, washed cheesecloth and place it over a deep bowl. Pour fruit and its rendered juice into the bag or lined colander and let the mixture drain. This will take about 3 to 4 hours. For sparkling clear jelly, let the juice drip undisturbed into the bowl; do not squeeze the bag or cloth. Pressed juice will make cloudy jelly. **(Photo B.)**

5. *Cook the jelly.* Make jelly in small batches, cooking only 4 to 6 cups of juice at a time. *Do not double recipes.* Larger batches take longer to cook, are difficult to handle, and may refuse to jell. **(Photo C.)**

　　To make jelly with commerical pectin, follow the recipe or package directions and proceed to Step 6.

　　To make jelly without additional pectin, use only high-pectin fruits (see chart, page 21), and follow a recipe or use the following directions as a guide. Measure the juice into a deep kettle and add lemon juice if necessary to give the juice a mildly tart flavor. (See Acid Test, page 20.) Bring the juice to a boil and add 3/4 to 1 cup of sugar per cup of juice. Stir to dissolve. Boil the juice in an uncovered pot until it reaches the jell point. Test for a jell. (See below.)

　　When making jelly without additional pectin, it is particularly important to cook the fruit juice long enough and at a high enough temperature so that it will jell to a "jiggly" firmness when cooled. Also it is essential not to overcook the mixture. Little can be done to improve the consistency and flavor of an overcooked mixture. Signs of overcooking are a change in the color of the mixture and the taste or odor of caramelized sugar. On the next page we describe how to test jelly for doneness. ⟶

D

E

adjoining column). Add 2/3 cup homemade pectin stock to every 4 cups of low- or medium-pectin fruit juice. Test for pectin content again. Juices very low in pectin may require additional homemade pectin stock. Bring the juice to a boil, add 3/4 to 1 cup of sugar per cup of juice, and stir to dissolve. Boil juice rapidly until it reaches the jell point. Test for a jell.

To test the pectin content of juice, add 1 tablespoon of strained juice to 1 tablespoon of rubbing alcohol. Stir to mix. (*Do not taste*; rubbing alcohol is poisonous.) Juice rich in pectin will clot into a jelly-like mass that can be picked up with a fork. Juice low in pectin will remain liquid or form only a few jelly-like clumps. **(Photo E.)**

6. *Fill the jars.* Once the jelly has reached the jell point, remove the pot from the heat and, with a long-handled spoon, quickly and carefully skim off any surface scum that might cloud the jelly. Immediately ladle jelly into hot, sterilized jars, leaving 1/8-inch headspace when using jars with metal lids and ring bands and 1/4-inch headspace when sealing with paraffin wax.

7. *Seal the jars.* Seal the jars with paraffin wax or with metal lids and ring bands.

To seal with paraffin, melt the wax in a disposable container (such as a clean soup can) set in a pan of hot water. *Never melt paraffin over direct heat—it is highly flammable.* **(Photo F.)**

After the jelly has been ladled into sterilized containers, immediately pour a *thin* layer (1/8-inch deep) of melted paraffin over it. Grasp the hot jar with a pot holder and rotate it slowly so the paraffin will cling to the sides of the container. Prick any air bubbles that appear in the paraffin before they have time to set. (Air bubbles will cause the seal to break.) Cool jars or glasses on a cooling rack or folded towel in a draft-free place until the jelly is cool and the paraffin sets. As the paraffin cools, it will harden, become opaque, and sink slightly in the center. **(Photo G.)**

Label containers and cover them tightly to prevent dust from settling in the paraffin. Commercial jelly glasses have colorful lids for this purpose, but plastic wrap or a cloth anchored with string or a rubber band works well.

The most dependable way to tell when jelly has reached doneness (commonly referred to as the jell point) is with an accurate candy, jelly, or deep-fat thermometer. First, take the temperature of boiling water. (The boiling point will vary depending on the altitude and may change with atmospheric conditions.) Then, cook the jelly mixture to a temperature 8°F higher than your boiling point. The temperature to reach at sea level is 220°F. At this point, enough liquid has evaporated from the juice mixture to concentrate the sugar, acid, and pectin and transform it into jelly.

You also can test for the jell point by dipping a cool metal spoon into the boiling liquid. Lift the spoon out and tip it so that the jelly runs off the side of the spoon. When the jelly falls in two drops and then flows together to form a sheet, it is ready. **(Photo D.)**

When the jell point is still in question, put a spoonful of jelly onto a cold plate and place it in the freezer for a few minutes. The mixture will set if the jell point has been reached. Remember to remove the kettle from the heat while you perform this test.

To make jelly with homemade pectin stock, follow the recipes on pages 25 and 28, or use these directions as a guide. Measure the juice into a deep pot and add lemon juice, if necessary, to give the juice a mildly tart flavor. (See Acid Test, page 20.) Test for the pectin content (see

To seal with metal lids, after the jelly has been ladled into jars, wipe the jar rims clean, place lids on the jars with the sealing compound next to the glass, and screw on the metal bands. Some older recipes call for inverting the jars briefly to help seal them and to kill bacteria that may be on the lid. This practice is no longer recommended by the U.S. Department of Agriculture or by jar manufacturers.

Cool the jars on a cooling rack or folded towel in a draft-free place. Leave space between the jars for air to circulate. To test the seal on metal lids, press the center of each with your finger. Lids will stay down when they're sealed.

Store jelly in a cool, dark, dry place. Jellies sealed with paraffin wax need to be stored at a temperature of 32° to 50°F to prevent mold and bacterial growth. Once opened, jars must be refrigerated.

JELLIES

You'll be rewarded with delicious jellies when you follow any of the recipes in this section. Try a variety—those made with different forms of commercial pectin, and those without—and experiment with homemade pectin stock. Once you get the hang of jelly-making, you'll develop the confidence and ability to improvise. With a little practice, you'll be producing delightfully different jellies that are uniquely your own, and far superior to store-bought products.

Lemon Honey Jelly

Give jelly a new twist with the natural taste of your favorite mild honey. This jelly is a perfect complement to whole-grain breads.

2-1/2 cups mild honey

3/4 cup fresh strained lemon juice

Grated peel of 2 lemons (optional)

1 pouch (3 oz) liquid fruit pectin

1. Place honey, lemon juice, and lemon peel in 6-quart or larger pot. Bring to a full boil, stirring constantly.

2. Add pectin and bring to a full, rolling boil, stirring constantly.

3. Boil rapidly 1 minute. Remove pan from heat and continue stirring for 3 minutes.

4. Quickly ladle into hot, sterilized jars, leaving 1/8-inch headspace; seal.

Yield: 4 half-pints.

Sweet Plum Jelly

Flavorful, sweet plums are abundant throughout the country during the summer months. Double your bounty by turning their juice into jelly and their pulp into creamy plum butter. (See page 39.)

4 pounds sweet plums

1 cup water

1/4 cup lemon juice

2/3 cup homemade apple pectin stock (page 22)

3-3/4 cups sugar

1. To extract juice from plums: Wash and pit plums but do not peel. Cut plums into pieces. Place plums in a 6-quart or larger pot and crush fruit to start juices flowing. Pour water over plums, cover, and bring to a boil. Simmer for about 20 minutes, stirring occasionally, until plums have rendered their juices. Do not overcook plums.

2. Pour juice and pulp through a damp jelly bag or cheesecloth-lined colander. Allow to drip undisturbed for several hours.

3. Measure 3-1/2 cups plum juice into a 6-quart or larger pot. (Reserve pulp for making plum butter or discard.)

4. Add lemon juice and pectin stock. Bring juice mixture to a boil.

5. Stir in sugar and return to a full boil over high heat. Boil rapidly, stirring occasionally, until mixture reaches the jell point. Test for jell point.

6. Remove jelly from heat and skim off foam with metal spoon.

7. Ladle quickly into hot, sterilized jars, leaving 1/8-inch headspace; seal.

Yield: 4 half-pints.

During July and August make ripe currants into jelly. Heated into a syrup it makes a brilliant glaze for berry tarts.

Red Currant Jelly

Every year we wait for a few precious jars of currant jelly to arrive in the mail from Iowa —a state where the currant bush thrives. If currants grow near you, capture their essence in a sweet-tart jelly— the next best thing to eating them straight from the bush.

3-1/2 quarts (about 4 lb) ripe currants

1 cup water

7 cups sugar

1 pouch (3 oz) liquid fruit pectin

1. Wash currants and remove large stems. Crush berries in a 6-quart pot and add water. Cover, bring to a boil, and simmer for 10 minutes.

2. Pour juice and pulp into a damp jelly bag or cheesecloth-lined colander and allow juice to drip undisturbed into a bowl for several hours.

3. Measure 5 cups juice into a 6-quart or larger pot. Stir in sugar and bring to a boil, stirring constantly.

4. All at once, stir in liquid pectin. Bring to a full, rolling boil and boil rapidly for 1 minute.

5. Remove from heat and skim off foam with a metal spoon.

6. Ladle quickly into hot, sterilized jars, leaving 1/8-inch headspace; seal.

Yield: 7 half-pints.

Apple-Grape Jelly

Grapes and tart apples make a perfect marriage of flavors and pectin levels. The resulting jelly is a versatile complement to everything from toast to wild game.

4 pounds Concord grapes (slightly underripe), stemmed

3 tart apples, stemmed and very thinly sliced

1/2 cup water

2 tablespoons lemon juice

4 cups sugar

1. Place grapes in a bowl and crush. Do not peel or core apples. Place grapes, sliced apples, and water in a 6- to 8-quart pot and bring to a boil. Reduce heat and simmer, covered, for 20 to 25 minutes or until grapes and apples render their juices. Pour juice and pulp through a damp jelly bag or cheesecloth-lined colander and let drip undisturbed into a large bowl for several hours.

2. Re-strain the juice slowly through a damp jelly bag or layers of damp cheesecloth to remove tartrate crystals that have settled in bottom of bowl. Reserve the pulp for grape butter if desired.

3. Measure 5 cups of grape-apple juice and the lemon juice into a 6-quart or larger pot and bring to a full boil over high heat.

4. Stir in sugar, return to a full, rolling boil, and continue cooking until the jell point is reached.

5. Remove from heat and immediately skim off foam with metal spoon.

6. Ladle quickly into hot, sterilized jars, leaving 1/8-inch headspace; seal.

Yield: 4 half-pints.

Note: This recipe will yield enough pulp for 4 half-pints of grape butter. See page 39 for instructions.

Apple Jelly

Tart apples, high in natural pectin, produce a mild-flavored jelly that is wonderful just plain or infused with the essence of herbs.

3 pounds apples

3 cups water

2 tablespoons strained lemon juice

3 cups sugar

1. To prepare and extract juice: Select one-fourth firm-ripe and three-fourths fully ripe tart apples. Wash and remove stems and blossom ends; do not pare or core. Cut apples into small pieces and place in an 8-quart pot. Add water, cover, and bring to a boil on high heat. Reduce heat and simmer for 20 minutes or until apples are soft and have rendered their juices. Pour pulp and juice into damp jelly bag or cheesecloth-lined colander and let drip undisturbed for 4 hours or overnight.

2. Measure 4 cups of apple juice into a 6-quart or larger pot. Add lemon juice and sugar and stir well. Bring to a boil.

3. Boil until juice reaches the jell point. (See page 24.) Stir occasionally to prevent sticking and scorching.

4. Remove from heat and skim off foam with spoon.

5. Quickly ladle into hot, sterilized jars, leaving 1/8-inch headspace; seal.

Yield: 3 to 4 half-pints.

Herb Jelly: To flavor apple jelly with a fresh herb, tie about 20 sprigs of the herb (rosemary, tarragon, mint, basil, thyme, or sage) in a small cheesecloth bag. Place the bag in the pot of boiling Apple Jelly after Step 2. Remove it when the jell point is reached and proceed as directed.

Enter your favorite jam, jelly, or preserve recipe in the county fair or other recipe contest.

Juanita's Beet Jelly

The next time you cook fresh beets, consider treating yourself to this delicious amber jelly made from leftover cooking liquid. The lemon juice and sugar transform this vegetable juice into a sparkling, fruit-flavored jelly. It is perfect on biscuits, toast, or muffins.

8 or more beets

5 cups water

1/2 cup lemon juice

1 package powdered pectin

6 cups sugar

1. Peel beets and simmer in water for 30 minutes.

2. When beets are tender, strain off cooking liquid. Measure 4 cups beet juice into a 6-quart or larger pot.

3. Stir in lemon juice and pectin. Bring to a boil over high heat, stirring constantly.

4. All at once stir in the sugar. Bring to a full, rolling boil and boil rapidly for 1 minute, stirring constantly.

5. Remove jelly from heat; skim off foam with a metal spoon.

6. Ladle quickly into hot, sterilized jars, leaving 1/8-inch headspace; seal.

Yield: 4 to 6 half-pints.

Mint Jelly

1 cup chopped, solidly packed mint leaves and tender stems

1 cup water

1/2 cup cider vinegar

3-1/2 cups sugar

5 drops green food coloring (optional)

1 pouch (3 oz) liquid fruit pectin

1. Put chopped mint into a 6-quart pot. Add water, vinegar, and sugar; stir well.

2. Place on high heat and, stirring constantly, bring quickly to a full, rolling boil that cannot be stirred down.

3. Add food coloring (if desired) and pectin.

4. Return to a full, rolling boil. Boil rapidly for 30 seconds.

5. Remove from heat. Skim off foam with a metal spoon. Strain immediately through two thicknesses of damp cheesecloth.

6. Ladle jelly quickly into hot, sterilized jars, leaving 1/8-inch headspace; seal.

Yield: 3 to 4 half-pints.

Crabapple Jelly

3 pounds crabapples

3 cups water

4 cups sugar

1. Select firm, crisp fruit, about one-fourth slightly underripe and the rest fully ripe. Sort, wash, and remove stems and blossom ends. Do not pare or core. Cut apples into small pieces and place in a 6-quart or larger pot.

2. Add water, cover, and bring to a boil on high heat. Reduce heat and simmer, covered, for 20 minutes or until crabapples are soft.

3. Place fruit pulp and juice in a damp jelly bag or a cheesecloth-lined colander and allow juice to drip undisturbed into a bowl for 3 to 4 hours or overnight.

4. Measure 4 cups of juice into a 6-quart or larger pot.

5. Add sugar and stir well. Bring to a boil over high heat. Boil rapidly, stirring occasionally, until mixture reaches the jell point. (See page 24.)

6. Remove from heat; skim off foam with a metal spoon.

7. Ladle quickly into hot, sterilized jars or glasses, leaving 1/8-inch headspace; seal.

Yield: 5 to 6 half-pints.

Jalapeño Pepper Jelly

Recipients of a jar of this jelly will be so charmed they'll want to be on your gift list permanently. This jelly looks striking when made with red bell peppers and makes a delightful hors d'oeuvre when spread on crackers with cream cheese. It's also good as an accompaniment to barbecued meats or spread on corn bread.

3 to 5 fresh jalapeño peppers, stemmed and seeded

4 medium-size bell peppers

1 cup white vinegar

5 cups sugar

2 pouches (3 oz each) liquid fruit pectin

1. Grind jalapeño and bell peppers in a food chopper or food processor, or mince with a knife.

2. Combine ground peppers and their juices, vinegar, and sugar in a 6-quart or larger pot; bring to a slow boil and boil 10 minutes.

3. Remove from heat and stir in pectin. Return to heat and bring to a boil; boil rapidly for 1 minute.

4. Remove from heat and skim off foam with a metal spoon.

5. Quickly ladle into hot, sterilized jars, leaving 1/8-inch headspace; seal.

Yield: 5 half-pints.

Strawberry Jelly

This recipe is an example of how apple pectin stock can be combined with low-pectin strawberry juice to produce perfect jelly. The flavor of freshly picked strawberries predominates.

5 pounds (about 7 pint baskets) strawberries

Water

1-1/2 cups homemade apple pectin stock (more if needed) (page 22)

4 cups sugar

1. Wash and hull berries. Place in a 6-quart or larger pot and crush berries to start the juices flowing.

2. Place over low heat, adding just enough water to keep the fruit from sticking and scorching until the juices begin to flow. Simmer slowly for 10 minutes.

3. Pour juice and pulp through a damp jelly bag or cheesecloth-lined colander and let drain into a bowl for several hours.

4. Measure 4 cups of juice into a 6-quart pot.

5. Add the homemade pectin stock, stir, and test for pectin level. (See page 24.) If the pectin is insufficient, add more pectin stock and retest. Very ripe berries may require up to 1 cup of pectin stock to each cup of juice.

6. Stir in sugar and bring to a boil over high heat. Boil rapidly, stirring occasionally, until jell point is reached. Test for jell point. (See page 24.)

7. Remove jelly from heat and skim off foam with a metal spoon.

8. Ladle quickly into hot, sterilized jars, leaving 1/8-inch headspace; seal.

Yield: 4 half-pints.

Wine Jelly

Although any wine can be used to make jelly, the best wines are those with full body and flavor. For deep red jelly, try a ruby port or a robust red wine. For a soft rose-colored jelly, choose a fruity rosé such as Grenache Rosé. White table wines best suited for jelly-making are those with a faintly sweet or fruity flavor, like Gewürztraminer. Berry or other fruit wines may also be used.

Wine jellies that will be used within a few months can be made in wine glasses or inexpensive dessert dishes and sealed with paraffin. These sparkling, jewel-colored jellies make lovely gifts.

2 cups wine

3 cups sugar

1 pouch (3 oz) liquid fruit pectin

1. Mix wine and sugar in top of double boiler over rapidly boiling water.

2. Cook, stirring constantly, about 3 minutes or until sugar is completely dissolved.

3. Remove double boiler from heat, but let jelly remain over hot water. At once stir in liquid pectin and mix well.

4. Skim off foam with a metal spoon.

5. Quickly ladle into hot, sterilized jars or glasses, leaving 1/4-inch headspace; seal.

Note: If using wine glasses, place a metal spoon in each hot glass before pouring in hot jelly, to keep glass from breaking. Seal with a thin layer of paraffin.

Yield: About 4 half-pints.

Two-Toned Wine Jelly:

Small, slender glasses show off two-toned jelly. Make one batch of white-wine jelly and one of red- or rosé-wine jelly. Fill half the glass with white-wine jelly. When it has set, pour on red- or rosé-wine jelly. Seal glasses with a thin layer of paraffin. Yield, about 8 half-pints.

January Jelly

When fresh fruits are out of season, you can still fill your pantry with homemade jellies simply by reaching into your freezer.

1 cup water

3-1/4 cups sugar

3 tablespoons strained lemon juice

1 pouch (3 oz) liquid fruit pectin

1 can (6 oz or 3/4 cup) frozen concentrated orange or orange-and-grapefruit juice, thawed

1. Place water in a 6-quart or larger pot and stir in sugar.

2. Place on high heat and, stirring constantly, bring quickly to a full, rolling boil. Add lemon juice. Boil rapidly for 1 minute.

3. Remove from heat. Stir in pectin. Add juice concentrate and mix well.

4. Skim off foam with a metal spoon, if necessary.

5. Ladle quickly into hot, sterilized jars, leaving 1/8-inch headspace; seal.

Yield: 4 half-pints.

Wine jellies look stunning in wine glasses sealed with paraffin. For a novel effect, layer red and white jellies together.

BREADS

Bake these delicious fresh breads to go with your homemade jellies, jams, and preserves. We've featured a variety from the cake-like French Brioche to the nutty, slightly sweet Best-Ever Bran Muffin. Every one will surely satisfy your craving for home-baked bread smothered with your favorite preserves.

Whole Wheat Bread

    5 cups all-purpose flour
    2 packages active dry yeast
2-3/4 cups water
    1/2 cup firmly packed brown sugar
    1/4 cup margarine
      1 tablespoon salt
      3 cups whole wheat flour

1. In a large bowl combine 3-1/2 cups of the all-purpose flour and yeast.

2. In saucepan heat water, brown sugar, margarine, and salt until warm (110° to 115°F), stirring constantly to melt margarine. Add to dry ingredients; beat with electric mixer 4 minutes.

3. By hand stir in whole wheat flour and enough of the remaining all-purpose flour to make a moderately stiff dough.

4. Turn onto a lightly floured surface and knead until smooth and elastic, about 10 to 12 minutes.

5. Shape into a ball. Place ball in lightly greased bowl, turning to grease surface. Cover and let rise in a warm place until double (about 1 hour).

6. Punch dough down; turn out onto lightly floured surface. Divide in half. Cover and let rest 10 minutes.

7. Shape dough into two loaves and place in two greased 9×5×2-1/2-inch loaf pans.

8. Cover and let rise in a warm place until almost double (about 45 minutes).

9. Bake at 375°F for 40 to 45 minutes. If necessary, cover loosely with foil the last 20 minutes of baking to prevent overbrowning.

10. Remove from pans and cool on wire racks.

Yield: 2 loaves.

Grape Bread: Divide the dough in half and weigh thirteen 2-ounce balls, a 1-ounce stem, tendrils, and a leaf. Arrange on a greased baking sheet to resemble a grape cluster. (Grape balls should be barely touching— do not crowd.) Cover and let rise until almost double (45 minutes). Bake at 375°F for 25 to 30 minutes.

Raised Biscuits

    1 package active dry yeast
    1 tablespoon sugar
    2 tablespoons warm water
    2 cups all-purpose flour
    1 teaspoon *each* baking powder and salt
    2 tablespoons butter
2/3 cup buttermilk

1. In small bowl combine yeast, sugar, and water; let stand until bubbly, about 15 minutes.

2. In a large bowl, stir together flour, baking powder, and salt. Cut in butter to make a fine crumb.

3. Beat in yeast mixture and buttermilk to make a moderately stiff dough. (Add more flour if necessary.)

4. Knead dough lightly for a few seconds on floured board.

5. Pat out to 1/2-inch thickness. Cut dough with a 2-inch floured biscuit cutter.

6. Arrange biscuits in a greased baking pan so they barely touch each other; prick tops with a fork.

7. Let rise in a warm place until doubled (30 to 40 minutes).

8. Bake at 425°F for 10 to 15 minutes or until golden.

Yield: 10 to 12.

Brioche

    1/2 cup butter, at room temperature
    1/3 cup sugar
      1 teaspoon salt
    3/4 cup hot (120°F) tap water
    1/4 cup nonfat dry milk
      1 package active dry yeast
      3 eggs, at room temperature
      1 egg yolk
3-1/2 cups all-purpose flour
      1 egg white

1. Cream butter, sugar, and salt in a large bowl.

2. Stir in water, dry milk, yeast, eggs, egg yolk, and 1-1/2 cups flour. Beat with an electric mixer at medium speed for 3 minutes.

3. By hand stir in the balance of the flour—2 cups—and beat vigorously for 3 minutes.

4. Cover bowl with plastic wrap and let dough rise in a warm place until doubled (about 2 hours).

5. Stir dough down and beat with a wooden spoon for 2 minutes.

6. Replace plastic wrap and refrigerate 4 hours or overnight.

7. Punch dough down and shape. Cover with wax paper and place in a warm place until doubled (30 to 40 minutes).

8. Brush with egg white beaten with a little water. Bake in one of the ways directed below.

Brioche Loaves: Divide dough equally into thirds and shape into loaves. Place in three greased mini loaf pans (5-1/2×2-1/2 inches). Let rise until doubled. Bake at 375°F for 30 to 35 minutes. Makes 3 small loaves.

Petites Brioches: Divide dough into 24 equal pieces. Dough is easiest to handle if kept cold, so shape a few pieces at a time, keeping remaining pieces covered separately and refrigerated until ready to use.

Pinch off about one-eighth of each portion and set aside. Shape larger section into a smooth ball by pulling surface of dough to underside of ball. Set ball, smooth side up, in a well-buttered 3- to 4-inch petite brioche pan or 3-inch muffin cup. Press dough down to fill pan bottom evenly. Shape small piece into a teardrop that is smooth on top.

With your finger, poke a hole in the center of brioche dough and insert pointed end of teardrop-shaped piece of dough, setting it in securely. Cover and let rise. Paint top lightly with egg white glaze. Bake at 375°F for 15 to 20 minutes or until richly browned. Remove from pans and serve warm or let cool on racks. Makes 2 dozen.

Top, left to right: Rosie's Jam Roll, Best-Ever Bran Muffins, Whole Wheat Bread. Bottom, left to right: Grape Bread, Raised Biscuits, Brioche.

Best-Ever Bran Muffins

1/4 cup butter or
  margarine
1/2 cup firmly packed
  brown sugar
1/4 cup light molasses
  2 eggs
  1 cup milk
1-1/2 cups bran
  1 cup all-purpose flour
1-1/2 teaspoons baking
  soda
3/4 teaspoon salt

1. In a medium bowl cream butter and sugar on low speed of electric mixer. Add molasses and eggs and beat well.

2. Mix in milk, then bran.

3. Combine flour, baking soda, and salt; stir in until just blended.

4. Divide among paper-lined muffin tins and bake at 400°F for15 minutes.

Yield: 15 muffins.

Rosie's Jam Roll

  1 package active dry
    yeast
  2 tablespoons warm
    water
  1 tablespoon sugar
1-3/4 cups flour
    (approximately)

1/2 teaspoon salt
1/2 cup sweet butter, cut
  in small pieces
  1 egg
1/4 cup sour cream
1/2 cup jam

1. In small bowl combine yeast and water; stir in sugar. Set aside.

2. In bowl or food processor combine flour and salt and cut in butter until mixture resembles coarse meal.

3. Beat egg with sour cream; stir into yeast mixture, then beat liquid into flour mixture. If necessary, add more flour to make a nonsticky dough.

4. Wrap and refrigerate several hours or overnight.

5. Roll chilled pastry into a 12×16-inch rectangle on floured board. Spread jam over dough to within 1/2 inch of edges.

6. Roll, jelly roll fashion, from shorter side. Turn ends under and place seam side down on greased baking sheet.

7. Bake at 350°F for 30 minutes. Turn oven off and leave in oven an additional 5 minutes. Cool on rack.

Yield: 1 roll; 15 to 20 slices.

How to Make Jams and Other Fruit Preserves

Jams, preserves, conserves, marmalades, and fruit butters glow with the natural color and flavor of fresh fruit.

Jams and most other fruit preserves are all made in about the same manner, with a few variations on the basic theme. Fruit butters are the exception; their cooking process is explained on page 39. Jams, preserves, conserves, and marmalades are cooked to the jell point, the point at which the fruit thickens and jells. For fruit preserves other than jelly, the jell point is 9°F (jelly is 8°F) higher than the boiling point of water. If you don't have a thermometer, the refrigerator test suggested for jelly-making (page 24) may be used.

If pectin is called for in a recipe, usually its purpose is to speed the cooking process or to ensure that fruit preserves made from low-pectin fruits jell properly. We prefer fruit preserves made without pectin; they are fruitier, richer in color, and slightly softer. Manufacturers of com-

mercial pectin, of course, call for using additional pectin, so to satisfy everyone, we're presenting recipes both with and without additional pectin. Remember that powdered and liquid pectin are not interchangeable.

Jam is the simplest of all fruit preserves to make. Fruit is crushed and then boiled with sugar in its own juice until it is reduced to a thick, spreadable consistency. Virtually all fleshy fruits make beautiful jams. Firmer fruits, such as apples and pears, are best saved for conserves. Most jams are made from a single fruit; however, blends of compatible fruits, such as peaches and plums or strawberries and rhubarb (a microwave jam recipe), are delightful.

As we mentioned before, the techniques for jam-making are similar to those for making preserves, conserves, and marmalades. We suggest that you familiarize yourself with the step-by-step jam-making procedure before trying any of the recipes.

A

B

Step-by-Step Method for Making Jam

1. *Prepare the jars.* Wash and rinse canning jars, lids, and rings. Allow the containers to remain in hot water or place in a low (200°F) oven until you're ready to use them. Scald lids and rings following manufacturer's directions. Leave the lids in the water until you're ready to use them.

2. *Prepare the fruit.* Wash fruit; remove stems, seeds, cores, and any bruised parts. Chop, slice, crush, or leave fruit whole as the recipe directs.

3. *Cook the fruit.* Measure the fruit into a large kettle.

For jam made without additional (commercial) pectin, bring the fruit and sugar to a boil and cook the mixture to a temperature 9°F higher than the boiling point of water. (Check the temperature of boiling water first; it will vary depending on your altitude and atmospheric conditions.) Cooking will take from 15 to 40 minutes depending on the amount of natural pectin in the fruit. Rather than cook low-pectin fruits too long, stop the cooking when they begin to thicken (they will thicken more as they cool) and be satisfied with soft jam, or use commercial pectin. **(Photo A.)**

For jam made with commercial pectin, follow the recipe or package directions.

4. *Fill and seal the jars.* Ladle hot jam through a wide-mouth funnel into clean, hot canning jars. Leave 1/4-inch headspace. Wipe jar rims clean, place lids on jars with sealing compound next to the glass, and screw the ring bands on firmly, but not too tightly. **(Photo B.)**

5. *Process the jars.* Place filled jars on a rack in a water-bath canner or deep, covered kettle filled with hot, but not boiling, water. Arrange jars on the rack so they do not touch each other or the sides of the canner. Add hot water as needed to cover the jar tops with an inch or two of water. Bring the water to a boil, and boil with the canner covered for 10 minutes. Start counting the processing time when the water reaches the boil. At altitudes above 3,000 feet, add 2 minutes' processing time for each additional 1,000 feet. Remove jars with a jar lifter and cool on a folded towel or rack in a draft-free place. Leave space between the jars for air to circulate.

6. *Test for a seal.* To test the seal, press down the center of each lid with your finger. Lids that are sealed will stay down.

Store jam and other preserves in a cool, dark, dry place. Once opened, fruit preserves should be stored in the refrigerator.

JAMS

The collection of recipes that follows will fill your pantry with long-time favorites, as well as some more unusual types of jams sure to delight your palate. Once you've mastered the principles of jam-making, you can venture further—substituting one fruit for another, adding spices or flavorings, combining ingredients in new ways—to create delectable jams tailored to your taste.

Strawberry Jam

This old-fashioned favorite has a fresh berry flavor and a clear, bright red color.

2 quarts crushed strawberries

3 tablespoons lemon juice

6 cups sugar

1. Measure berries and place in an 8-quart or larger pot.

2. Add lemon juice and sugar to berries; bring slowly to boiling, stirring occasionally until sugar dissolves.

3. Cook rapidly to the jell point (page 24) or until thick (about 30 minutes). As mixture thickens, stir frequently to prevent sticking.

4. Remove from heat and skim with a metal spoon to remove foam.

5. Quickly ladle into clean, hot jars, leaving 1/4-inch headspace; seal.

6. Process in boiling-water bath 10 minutes.

Yield: About 8 half-pints.

Rhubarb Ginger Jam

This jam will delight rhubarb lovers with its distinctive blend of flavors.

2 pounds fresh rhubarb, trimmed and sliced in 1-inch pieces

1/2 cup water

2 tablespoons lemon juice

A 1-inch piece of fresh ginger root, peeled and crushed

3 cups sugar

2 tablespoons finely chopped crystallized ginger

1. Combine rhubarb pieces, water, lemon juice, and crushed ginger root in an 8-quart or larger pot; bring to a boil. Reduce heat and simmer, stirring frequently, until the rhubarb is soft.

2. Add sugar and stir well to dissolve. Add crystallized ginger and bring to a boil. Boil rapidly, stirring frequently, to the jell point. (See page 24.)

3. Quickly ladle into clean, hot jars, leaving 1/4-inch headspace; seal.

4. Process in boiling-water bath 10 minutes.

Yield: 9 half-pints.

Blackberry Jam

Not only is this jam terrific on toast, it also makes a tasty topping for cheesecake, pound cake, or ice cream.

9 or 10 pint baskets blackberries (9 cups crushed)
6 cups sugar

1. Remove any stems from berries and crush. See note below if you wish to remove seeds.

2. Combine berries and sugar in a 6-quart or larger pot. Bring slowly to a boil, stirring occasionally until sugar dissolves.

3. Cook rapidly to, or almost to, jell point, depending upon whether a firm or a soft jam is desired. (See page 24.) As mixture thickens, stir frequently to prevent sticking.

4. Remove from heat and skim off foam with a metal spoon.

5. Ladle quickly into clean, hot jars, leaving 1/4-inch headspace; seal.

6. Process in boiling-water bath 10 minutes.

Yield: 6 to 8 half-pints.

Note: If seedless jam is preferred, crushed berries may be heated until soft and pressed through a sieve or put through a food mill; then add sugar and proceed as above. We usually remove the seeds from half of the berries.

Red Tomato Jam

This is a beautifully clear, red jam that uses fully or slightly overripe tomatoes. Make this toward the end of the season when tomatoes are ripening more quickly than you can use them.

3 pounds (about 6 large) fully ripe tomatoes

1 lemon, thinly sliced

1 package powdered fruit pectin

4 cups sugar

1. Scald, peel, and quarter tomatoes, removing stems and cores. Squeeze out seeds and juice, reserving only the pulp.

2. Bring the pulp to a boil in a large pot. Reduce heat and simmer, uncovered, for 8 to 10 minutes. Stir frequently to

prevent scorching. Measure pulp; there should be 3 cups.

3. Put tomatoes, lemon slices, and pectin in a 6-quart or larger pot. Bring to a full boil, stirring constantly. Add sugar and boil rapidly for another 2 minutes.

4. Cool for 5 minutes, stirring occasionally.

5. Quickly ladle into clean, hot jars, leaving 1/4-inch headspace; seal.

6. Process in boiling-water bath 10 minutes.

Yield: 4 half-pints.

Summer Peach Jam

This jam tastes like a bite of preserved summer sunshine.

5 pounds (about 12 large) firm-ripe peaches

3 tablespoons lemon juice

5 cups sugar

1. Wash, peel, and pit peaches. Slice peaches into small pieces. Measure 10 cups of sliced peaches.

2. Place peaches, lemon juice, and sugar in a large bowl and allow to sit for 1 hour.

3. Transfer peach mixture to an 8-quart or larger pot and simmer until the sugar is dissolved. Bring to a full boil.

4. Boil constantly until the jell point is reached (about 25 minutes). Stir occasionally at first and then constantly as the mixture nears the jell point. (See page 24.)

5. Remove from heat and skim off foam with a metal spoon.

6. Ladle quickly into clean, hot jars, leaving 1/4-inch headspace; seal.

7. Process in boiling-water bath 10 minutes.

Yield: 8 half-pints.

To: Sara
From: Aunt Susan

Preserve persimmons in the fall when they are available. Persimmon Jam and nut bread make a perfect combination.

Persimmon Jam

4 pounds (about 10) *very ripe* persimmons

4 cups sugar

1. Cut persimmons in half and scoop out pulp. Press fruit through a strainer, put through a food mill, or purée in a food processor.

2. Measure 4 cups pulp into a 4-1/2-quart pot. Add sugar and stir well.

3. Cook over low heat, stirring constantly, until thickened (about 30 minutes). Keep the fruit mixture below the boiling point or the jam will become bitter. Remember also, the jam will thicken on cooling.

5. Ladle jam into clean, hot jars, leaving 1/4-inch headspace; seal.

6. Process in boiling-water bath 10 minutes.

Yield: 6 to 7 quarts.

Raspberry Jam

2 pounds raspberries

3 cups sugar

Juice of 1 lemon

1. Rinse and mash berries. Place in a 6-quart or larger pot with sugar and slowly bring to a boil, stirring to dissolve sugar.

2. Boil for 20 to 30 minutes, stirring frequently to prevent sticking and scorching, until thickened. (Jam will thicken on cooling.) Add lemon juice at the end of cooking time.

3. Remove from heat and skim off foam with a spoon.

4. Ladle jam into clean, hot jars, leaving 1/4-inch headspace; seal.

5. Process in a boiling-water bath 10 minutes.

Yield: 4 to 5 half-pints.

Blueberry preserves is great as a topping on Sunday brunch waffles.

PRESERVES

Unlike the jam-making process in which lengthy cooking times are required to reduce the fruit to a thick consistency, when making preserves the fruit is cooked in a sugar syrup for only a short time to maintain as much of the natural color, flavor, and texture of the fruit as possible.

This process is perfect for strawberries, raspberries, and other thick-skinned berries because they retain their texture and form through the cooking process, and also render their juice to enrich the syrup. The reduction of the syrup to concentrate the juice flavor is the secret of making a sweet, flavorful preserve. Because the cooking process reduces and concentrates the fruit and syrup so much, the fruit will yield only about one-half its weight in preserves. Use preserves in the same way as jams and jellies.

Blueberry Preserves

Preserve the fresh blueberries of summer in a special blend of spices and cider vinegar.

    5 cups fresh blueberries, stemmed and washed

    2 tablespoons cider vinegar

2-1/4 cups sugar

    1/4 teaspoon *each* ground allspice and cinnamon

    1/8 teaspoon ground cloves

1. Combine blueberries with remaining ingredients in a 6-quart or larger pot.

2. Cook to the jell point (page 24) or until desired thickness is reached. Stir frequently.

3. Quickly ladle into clean, hot jars, leaving 1/4-inch headspace; seal.

4. Process in boiling-water bath 15 minutes.

Yield: About 5 half-pints.

Apricot Preserves

Don't miss apricots at the height of their short summer season. Fill crêpes or smother waffles with this marvelous preserve.

    2 pounds hard-ripe apricots

1/4 cup lemon juice

    4 cups sugar

1. Peel, halve, and pit apricots. You should have 5 cups.

2. Thoroughly mix fruit with lemon juice and sugar. Cover tightly; let stand for 4 to 5 hours in a cool place.

3. Heat the fruit mixture to boiling in a 6-quart or larger pot, stirring occasionally, until the sugar dissolves.

4. Cook rapidly until fruit is translucent (about 30 minutes). As mixture thickens, stir frequently to prevent sticking.

5. Quickly ladle into clean, hot jars, leaving 1/4-inch headspace; seal.

6. Process in boiling-water bath 15 minutes.

Yield: 4 half-pints.

Cherry Preserves

Don't let the birds eat all your beautiful ripe-red cherries! Preserve some of those sweet-tart fruits to enjoy on warm slices of toast and homemade muffins, or turn vanilla ice cream into a delicious sundae by spooning these preserves on top.

4 pounds tart, red cherries, pitted

4 cups sugar

1. Pit cherries over a bowl to catch juice. Drain juice from cherries and combine with sugar in a 6-quart or larger pot.

2. Cook over medium heat until sugar dissolves, stirring occasionally. (If there is not enough juice to dissolve sugar, add a little water.)

3. Add pitted cherries and cook rapidly until cherries become glossy (about 15 minutes).

4. Remove from heat; cover and let stand for 12 to 18 hours in a cool place.

5. Bring to boiling and cook rapidly 1 minute.

6. Quickly ladle into clean, hot jars, leaving 1/4-inch headspace; seal.

7. Process in boiling-water bath 15 minutes.

Yield: 4 half-pints.

CONSERVES

Conserves are a marriage of two or more fresh fruits, nuts, and often dried fruits, such as raisins. They are delicious as a spread or dessert topping, and are often tart and spicy enough to be served as a zesty accompaniment to meat or fowl.

When you prepare conserves, you may notice that dried fruits and nuts sometimes sink to the bottom of the cooking pot. To remedy this, allow the mixture to cool for about 5 minutes to thicken it slightly, then stir the mixture to distribute the ingredients evenly.

Also, be careful not to overcook conserves; they will become too thick and taste of caramel if you cook them past the jell point.

Apricot-Orange Conserve

Each fruit asserts its distinctive flavor, yet blends harmoniously in this delectable conserve.

3-1/2 cups chopped apricots (fresh, canned, or dried)

1-1/2 cups freshly squeezed orange juice (3 or 4 medium-size oranges)

Peel of 1/2 orange, finely grated

2 tablespoons lemon juice

3-1/2 cups sugar

1/2 cup chopped nuts

1. To prepare fresh apricots: wash, pit, and chop.

To prepare canned apricots: drain and chop apricots.

To prepare dried apricots: cook uncovered in 3 cups of water until tender (about 20 minutes); drain and chop.

2. Combine all ingredients except nuts in a 6-quart or larger pot. Cook to jell point (page 24) or until desired thickness is reached, stirring constantly.

3. Add nuts during last 5 minutes of cooking.

4. Remove from heat and skim off foam with a metal spoon.

5. Ladle into clean, hot jars, leaving 1/4-inch headspace; seal.

6. Process in boiling-water bath 15 minutes.

Yield: 5 to 6 half-pints.

Dried Fruit and Walnut Conserve

1/2 pound dried apricots (1-1/2 cups cut up)

1/2 pound dried peaches (1-1/3 cups cut up)

1/2 pound dried pears (1-1/3 cups cut up)

1/2 cup raisins

1 medium orange (1 cup chopped)

3 cups water

2 cups sugar

1 tablespoon lemon juice

1/2 teaspoon ground cinnamon

1/8 teaspoon ground cloves

1 cup chopped walnuts or other nuts

1. Chop dried fruits. Chop entire orange, including peel; discard seeds.

2. Combine dried fruits, orange, and water in an 8-quart or larger pot; cover and cook until fruits are tender (about 15 to 20 minutes).

3. Uncover and add remaining ingredients except nuts. Slowly bring to boiling, stirring occasionally, until sugar dissolves.

4. Cook rapidly, stirring frequently, until thick (about 10 minutes) or to the jell point (page 24). Add nuts the last 5 minutes of cooking.

5. Quickly ladle into clean, hot jars, leaving 1/4-inch headspace; seal.

6. Process in boiling-water bath 15 minutes.

Yield: About 5 half-pints.

Cranberry Conserve

Modify tradition a bit this year with this cranberry conserve. It's one less thing you'll have to prepare for busy holidays and it tastes terrific with turkey, chicken, or wild game.

1 unpeeled orange, very finely chopped

2 cups water

3 cups sugar

1 quart cranberries

1 cup raisins

1/2 cup chopped walnuts or other nuts

1. Combine orange and water in a 6-quart or larger pot; cook rapidly until peel is tender (about 20 minutes).

2. Add sugar, cranberries, and raisins. Bring slowly to boiling, stirring occasionally, until sugar dissolves.

3. Cook rapidly until mixture starts to thicken (about 8 minutes). As mixture thickens, stir frequently to prevent sticking. Stir in nuts the last 5 minutes of cooking.

4. Ladle into clean, hot jars, leaving 1/4-inch headspace; seal.

5. Process in boiling-water bath 15 minutes.

Yield: 4 half-pints.

Peach-Pineapple Conserve

Having a luau or simply baked ham or roast pork? This exotic conserve will lend a tropical touch.

    6 cups peeled, sliced ripe peaches

    4 cups sugar

1-1/2 cups cut-up pineapple (about 1/2 small pineapple or one 14-oz can tidbits)

    1 orange, finely chopped

    1 cup chopped walnuts or other nuts

1. Combine peaches and sugar; let stand until juice forms (about 1 hour).

2. If using fresh pineapple, peel, core, and remove brown spots; cut into small pieces. If using canned pineapple, be sure to drain.

3. Combine peach mixture, pineapple, and orange in a 6-quart or larger pot. Cook slowly, stirring occasionally, until thick (about 40 minutes) or to the jell point. (See page 24.)

4. Remove from heat and stir in nuts.

5. Quickly ladle into clean, hot jars, leaving 1/4-inch headspace; seal.

6. Process in boiling-water bath 15 minutes.

Yield: 6 half-pints.

Dried fruits and nuts create a beautiful marriage of rich flavors and colors. As a bonus, Dried Fruit and Walnut Conserve can be made and enjoyed the year around.

A

B

Step-by-Step Method for Making Fruit Butter

1. Wash and prepare fruit as directed above. You may use any quantity of fruit desired.

2. Cook fruit with water or in its own juice in large pot until soft.

3. Remove fruit from pan with a slotted spoon and put through food mill or press through a fine seive into bowl. Discard cooking liquid. (Photo A.)

4. Measure sieved pulp. Add 1/2 cup sugar to each cup pulp.

5. Add flavorings of your choice to taste.

6. Place fruit butter in a shallow (not more than 2 inches deep) glass, stainless steel, or enameled baking pan. Cook in a 300°F oven for 1-1/2 to 2-1/2 hours, stirring occasionally, until butter is thick and has a spreadable consistency. To test for doneness, place a spoonful on a chilled saucer. If no rim of liquid forms around edge of butter, it is done. (Photo B.)

7. Quickly ladle into clean, hot jars, leaving 1/4-inch headspace; seal.

8. Process in boiling-water bath 10 minutes.

Note: See page 41 for recipe for microwave Applesauce Butter.

How to Make Fruit Butters

Fruit butters are made by cooking the fruit until soft, putting it through a food mill, and cooking the pulp with sugar until it turns into a thick, creamy preserve. The step-by-step procedure on the following page demonstrates the method in detail.

Butters are quite economical; it's even possible to make them from the pulp that remains after extracting juice for jelly. In this section we show you how to turn left-over plum pulp from the recipe for Plum Jelly (page 25) into a creamy plum butter.

Although apple butter is the most common type of fruit butter, butters can be made from most fruits or fruit mixtures; fruits may also be blended for flavor and color. Use sound, ripe fruits or firm portions of windfalls or culls.

White or brown sugar may be used. Brown sugar darkens butters made from light fruits and adds a more pronounced flavor.

You may want to flavor your butters with some combination of spices, grated citrus peel or citrus juice, port wine, a liqueur, or an extract. Spice butters to taste or add a mixture of 1/4 teaspoon cinnamon and a pinch of ground allspice and of cloves per quart of butter. Ginger is good with pears— 1/4 to 1/2 teaspoon per quart of butter. For a light-colored butter, tie whole spices loosely in a cheesecloth bag; remove after butter is cooked.

Preparing Fruit for Butters

Apples: Peel, core, and slice or quarter. Cook with half as much water or apple cider as fruit or use a combination of the two liquids.

Apricots: Skin, pit, and crush fruit. Cook in its own juice or one-fourth as much water as fruit. Orange juice is also tasty.

Cantaloupe: Seed and peel, retaining juice. Chop or purée pulp. Cook in its own juice.

Crabapples: Quarter. Cook in one-fourth as much water as fruit.

Grapes: Remove stems, crush, and cook in own juice.

Mangoes: Use half-ripe mangoes. Peel and slice. Add 1 to 2 cups of water to every 6 cups of sliced fruit. Cook until soft enough to mash.

Nectarines: Peel and pit. Crush or slice fruit and cook in its own juice.

Peaches: Same as for nectarines.

Pears: Remove stems and blossom ends. Quarter and cook with half as much water as fruit.

Plums: Halve or quarter; pit. Crush and cook in own juice. With very small plums, pits will strain out.

Prunes (dried): Pit and cook prunes in a little water until soft.

Quince: Remove stems and blossom ends; cut into small pieces and cook with half as much water as fruit.

Rhubarb: Chop. Cook with 1/2 cup water to every 2 pounds fruit.

Amber Marmalade: (1) Cut outer peel in strips. (2) Remove pith from pulp.

MARMALADES

Marmalades contain the flesh and peel of citrus fruits, which impart a lovely bittersweet flavor and interesting texture and appearance. Some marmalades, such as Classic Orange Marmalade and Amber Marmalade, are based solely on citrus fruits. Others, such as Ginger Peach Marmalade, are a combination of citrus and other fruits.

Ginger-Peach Marmalade

This marmalade, more sweet than bitter, surprises the palate with undertones of fresh ginger root.

1 lemon

1 orange

1 quart water

4 pounds peaches

2 cups sugar

1 cup water

1 tablespoon peeled, finely chopped fresh ginger root

1. Using a sharp paring knife, remove the outer peel (colored part only) from the lemon and orange. Slice peel into very thin, short strips. Place peels in a pot, cover with 1 quart water, and simmer until tender (about 20 minutes).

2. Meanwhile, remove and discard the white portion of the peel from the lemon and orange.

3. Cut the citrus pulp into thin slices; halve or quarter each slice. Discard seeds.

4. Peel, pit, and chop peaches. To peel peaches, drop them for a few seconds into boiling water. Peel while still warm.

5. Combine peaches with citrus peel and set aside.

6. In a 6-quart or larger pot, combine sugar, 1 cup water, and ginger. Bring to a boil; reduce heat and simmer 5 minutes.

7. Add peaches, citrus peel, and citrus pulp; return to boil. Cook over medium heat 45 to 60 minutes, stirring frequently, until mixture thickens or reaches the jell point. (See page 24.)

8. Ladle quickly into clean, hot jars, leaving 1/4-inch headspace; seal.

9. Process in boiling-water bath 15 minutes.

Yield: 4 half-pints.

Amber Marmalade

Slivers of several kinds of citrus peel are swirled through this prize-winning marmalade.

    2 large oranges

    2 lemons

    2 grapefruits

    Water

    4 cups sugar (approximately)

1/8 teaspoon salt

1. Select thick-skinned citrus fruit with smooth, unblemished peel. Using a sharp paring knife, remove

Amber Marmalade, croissant, scrambled egg, and coffee.

outer citrus peel (colored part only) and cut into small, uniform strips. Reserve fruit pulp.

2. Place the slivered peels in a pot, add 2 quarts water, bring to a boil, and boil 5 minutes. Drain; discard water and reserve cooked peel.

3. Repeat Step 2.

4. Repeat Step 2 again. Be sure to reserve cooked peel.

5. Remove the white pith from the fruit pulp. Cut the pulp into thin slices, then cut slices into quarters and remove seeds.

6. Combine peel and pulp in a measuring cup, pressing fruit down before measuring. Place measured fruit in a 6-quart or larger pot. Add twice the amount of water as fruit pulp and peel.

7. Boil rapidly for about 30 minutes or until peel is tender.

8. Measure the fruit and liquid. Add an equal amount of sugar. Add salt.

9. Boil fruit, sugar, and salt rapidly for 10 to 20 minutes or until the mixture thickens, becomes amber colored, and reaches the jell point. (See page 24.) Stir occasionally at first and then constantly to prevent sticking or burning.

10. Remove from heat and skim off foam with a metal spoon.

11. Ladle into clean, hot jars, leaving 1/4-inch headspace; seal.

12. Process in boiling-water bath 10 minutes.

Yield: About 5 half-pints.

Classic Orange Marmalade

Traditionally, the finest orange marmalade is made from slightly bitter Seville oranges or sour oranges. They're hard to come by in this country, but if you can find Seville oranges, by all means use them in this recipe. They are in season from November to January. If you can't find bitter oranges, substitute sweet Valencia or navel oranges.

6 bitter oranges

2 sweet oranges

1 lemon

9-1/2 cups water

1-1/2 tablespoons strained fresh lemon juice

Sugar

1. Slice oranges and lemon very thinly. Remove and reserve seeds. Place the seeds in a small bowl with 1/2 cup of the water and set aside.

2. Place the lemon and orange slices in a large pot and cover with the remaining 9 cups water. Allow to soak for 24 hours.

3. Place pot containing orange and lemon slices over medium heat and simmer for about 35 minutes or until peel is tender. Remove from heat and allow to stand another 24 hours.

4. Measure the fruits and their liquid and return them to the pot, adding an equal amount of sugar. Bring to a boil and cook over medium heat, stirring frequently, until the jell point is reached (about 45 to 60 minutes).

5. Combine lemon juice and water strained from seeds, add to pot, and cook the marmalade 10 minutes more, stirring constantly.

6. Ladle into clean, hot jars, leaving 1/4-inch headspace; seal.

7. Process in boiling-water bath 15 minutes.

Yield: 8 half-pints.

Lime Marmalade

This homemade marmalade is every bit as good as the ones that are imported, but it's much less expensive.

10 limes (or 4 cups prepared limes)

12 cups cold water

12 cups sugar

1. With a very sharp paring knife, remove the outer green peel of the limes. Slice the peel into paper-thin strips and set aside. Slice the lime pulp very thinly and remove any seeds. Discard end slices. Measure the peel and the lime slices (you should have 4 cups) and cover with the cold water.

2. Allow this mixture to soak overnight.

3. The next day, place limes and liquid in an 8-quart or larger pot over moderate heat and cook, covered, for 20 minutes or until the lime rind is tender. Remove from heat and measure the cooked mixture. (You should have 12 cups.)

4. Add 12 cups sugar and stir over moderate heat until the sugar dissolves.

5. Boil rapidly, stirring frequently, until the marmalade reaches the jell point. (See page 24.)

6. Remove from heat and skim off foam with a metal spoon.

7. Ladle into clean, hot jars, leaving 1/4-inch headspace; seal.

8. Process in boiling-water bath 10 minutes.

Yield: 11 half-pints.

MICROWAVE FRUIT PRESERVES

Microwaving is the newest way of making fruit preserves. This method is both easy and quick, and the end product does not differ from its traditional counterpart. The following recipes have been developed by microwave oven manufacturers. They're sure to please everyone.

Strawberry-Rhubarb Jam

3 cups rhubarb, cut in 3/4-inch slices

2 cups sliced strawberries

2-1/2 cups sugar

1/8 teaspoon salt

1. Combine all ingredients in a 3-quart casserole. Cook in microwave oven, covered, on full power (high) for 5 minutes.

2. Remove cover. Cook in microwave oven on full power (high) for 30 to 40 minutes, or until jell point is reached. (See page 24.) Stir once or twice during cooking.

3. Remove from oven. Quickly ladle into clean, hot jars, leaving 1/4-inch headspace; seal.

4. Process in boiling-water bath 10 minutes.

Yield: 2 to 3 half-pints.

Applesauce Butter

Too busy to spend hours making apple butter? Prepare this easy microwave version in one-fourth the time or less.

4 cups (two 16-oz cans) applesauce

1 package powdered fruit pectin

1 tablespoon pumpkin pie spice

1 teaspoon cinnamon

4-1/2 cups sugar

1. In 3-quart casserole stir together applesauce, pectin, pumpkin pie spice, and cinnamon. Cover. Microwave at full power (high) for 8 to 10 minutes, stirring after 5 minutes, until mixture boils.

2. Add sugar to hot mixture, stirring well. Microwave at full power (high) 9 to 11 minutes, stirring twice at 5-minute intervals, until mixture reaches a full boil.

3. Boil 1 minute, stirring constantly.

4. Quickly ladle into clean, hot jars, leaving 1/4-inch headspace; seal.

5. Process in boiling-water bath 10 minutes.

Yield: 6 half-pints.

Cranberry Jelly

1 pound cranberries, washed and drained

2 cinnamon sticks

6 whole cloves

1/4 cup water

2 cups sugar

1-3/4 cups water

1. Combine cranberries, cinnamon sticks, cloves, and 1/4 cup water in a 2-quart casserole. Cook in microwave oven on full power (high) for 4-1/2 to 5 minutes or until cranberry skins burst. Stir halfway through cooking time.

2. Pour cranberries and juice through damp jelly bag or cheesecloth-lined colander, and let drip undisturbed into

Fruit Preserves—Problem Solver

Problem	Cause	Prevention
Formation of sugar crystals when making jelly	1. Too much sugar.	1. Prepare jellies with no more than ¾ to 1 cup sugar to each cup of juice.
	2. Undissolved sugar stuck to sides of kettle.	2a. After adding sugar, stir to dissolve completely.
		2b. Wipe sides of pan with a damp cloth to remove sugar crystals before filling jars.
	3. Jelly mixture was cooked too long or too slowly.	3. Cook at a rapid boil. Remove jelly from heat immediately when jell point is reached.
Synerisis, or "weeping," of jelly	1. Too much acid in juice made pectin unstable.	1. Taste juice for acidity—it should be mildly tart.
	2. Storage area was too warm or storage temperature fluctuated.	2. Store jellies in a cool, dark, dry place.
	3. Paraffin seal was too thick.	3. Seal jelly with a single layer of paraffin ⅛-inch deep.
Jelly too soft	1. Fruit was overcooked to extract juice.	1. Overcooking lowers the jelling ability of pectin.
	2. Too little sugar.	2. Prepare jellies with ¾ to 1 cup sugar per cup of juice.
	3. Too little acid.	3. Don't use overripe fruit. Add 1 tablespoon lemon juice to each cup of prepared juice that is low in acid. (See page 20.)
	4. Too large a batch made at once.	4. Use 4 to 6 cups of juice in each batch of jelly. Don't double recipes.
	5. Too little pectin.	5. See page 22 to rescue soft jelly with additional pectin.
Jelly too stiff or tough	1. Jelly mixture was overcooked.	1. Cook jelly mixture to a temperature 8°F higher than the boiling point of water. (See testing for a jell, page 24.)
	2. Too much pectin in fruit.	2. Use fully ripe fruit.
Cloudy jelly	1. Underripe fruit.	1. Use fully ripe fruit and supplement its natural pectin content with commercial or homemade pectin.
	2. Imperfect straining.	2. Don't squeeze juice, but let it drip undisturbed through a jelly bag.
	3. Jelly was allowed to stand before it was poured or was poured into jars slowly.	3. Pour jelly into jars immediately once the jell point is reached. Work quickly.
Bubbles in jelly and jam	Jelly was poured slowly into jars and air became trapped.	Hold the jars close to the kettle and ladle jelly quickly into jars.
Mold on fruit preserves	1. Jars were sealed incorrectly.	1. Follow methods outlined in the step-by-step procedure to ensure an airtight seal.
	2. Lack of proper sanitation.	2. Boil jelly containers in water 15 minutes to sterilize. Use clean, hot jars for other preserves.
Faded fruit preserves	Storage area too warm; jars exposed to light.	Store jars in a cool, dark place.

a bowl for 3 or 4 hours. Discard pulp and spices.

3. Return juice to casserole. Add sugar and 1-3/4 cups water. Mix well. Cook in microwave oven on full power (high) for 7 to 9 minutes, or until the mixture has boiled 3 to 4 minutes. Stir once or twice during the cooking time to keep mixture from boiling over. Remove from oven. Test for jell point. (See page 24.)

4. Skim off foam with a metal spoon.

5. Quickly pour into hot, sterilized jars, leaving 1/8-inch headspace; seal.

Yield: 4 half-pints.

Microwave Port Wine Conserve

Serve with roast meats or as a topping for French vanilla ice cream.

1-1/2 cups port wine

1 cup chopped raisins

3 cups sugar

3 large cinnamon sticks

1 tablespoon grated orange peel

1/4 teaspoon whole cloves

1/2 teaspoon ground cardamom

1 pouch (3 oz) liquid fruit pectin

1. In 3-quart casserole, stir together port, raisins, and sugar.

2. Prepare spice bag by placing cinnamon sticks, orange peel, cloves, and cardamom on a square of cheesecloth. Fold cloth around contents and tie securely with string. Add bag to wine mixture, stir, and let stand 5 minutes.

3. Microwave 8 to 10 minutes on full power (high), just until bubbles appear around edge. Stir well after 5 minutes. Do not boil.

4. Remove from microwave. Remove spice bag. Immediately stir pectin into hot mixture.

5. Quickly ladle into clean, hot jars, leaving 1/4-inch headspace; seal.

6. Process in boiling-water bath 15 minutes.

Yield: 3 to 4 half-pints.

Canning Fruits, Tomatoes, and Juices

Abundant fruits at the peak of their season are perfect for canning. In a short time you can stock your pantry with their good, wholesome flavors so they can be savored the year 'round.

When orchards, berry bushes, and tomato vines are laden with ripe, sweet-smelling fruits, it's the perfect time to set aside a few hours to capture their fresh flavor and texture for enjoyment later, when trees are bare and fresh produce is expensive.

Begin in the spring when tender pink stalks of rhubarb first appear, then add to your storehouse of canned goods throughout the summer and fall as each fruit reaches its peak. For a listing of the harvest seasons of different fruits and vegetables, see page 7.

Except for citrus fruits (other than grapefruit) and strawberries, most fruits can be canned successfully. Citrus fruits become bitter, and strawberries fade and lose their shape and texture when canned. You'll have better results turning citrus fruits into marmalades and making jellies and jams from strawberries.

As we discussed in "A Short Course on Canning," page 16, two heat-processing methods are used to can foods: the boiling-water bath method and the steam pressure method. The method used depends on the amount of acid in the food being canned. Unlike vegetables and meats, fruits, tomatoes, and fruit juices contain sufficient amounts of natural acid to inhibit the deterioration caused by spoilage organisms. As a result, they may be safely preserved by boiling the filled jars for a specified length of time in a water-bath canner.

The length of time fruit is processed depends on its density, its temperature when processing begins, and the size of its container. Small berries need less processing time than firm pear halves. Fruit packed raw into jars takes longer to reach the temperature needed to inactivate and destroy spoilage organisms than fruit that is packed hot. And fruit packed into quart jars requires longer processing than fruit packed into pints.

In addition to providing step-by-step instructions for canning almost every type of fruit, this chapter tells you how to can tomatoes. Packed into jars at the height of the season, vine-ripened tomatoes will lend garden-fresh flavor to soups, sauces, and stews throughout the year. You'll find tantalizing recipes for homemade tomato sauce, marinara sauce, and tomato paste on page 49.

This chapter also includes recipes for home-canned fruit sauces, fillings such as apple pie filling, and cranberry sauce. We also suggest ways to add variety to your canned fruits with spices or liqueurs. An abundance of fruit also suggests preservation as juices. A variety of recipes, from Apple Juice to Vegetable Juice Cocktail, begin on page 51. Open a jar to drink on a cold winter morning or use as a base for dessert sauces and blender drinks.

Preparing Fruits and Tomatoes for Canning

When you're ready to start canning, wash the fruit thoroughly; then work quickly to peel, core, and cut it. Avoid long periods of soaking and standing.

Fruit may be canned whole, halved, or sliced. You can leave the skins on whole fruits such as plums or fresh prunes, but prick them before packing to prevent bursting. Halved and sliced fruit, and whole fruits such as peaches and tomatoes, should be peeled. To peel easily, dip fruit in boiling water for about 30 seconds, plunge into cold water, and slip the skins off.

Fruits such as apples, apricots, peaches, and pears darken when they are cut. To prevent this, dip the cut fruit into a solution of 2 tablespoons vinegar, 2 tablespoons salt, and 1 gallon of water. (This solution may affect the fruit's flavor, so rinse the fruit before packing it into jars.) You also can use commercial powdered ascorbic acid, mixing 3 tablespoons powder into 2 quarts water.

Opposite:
Pouring syrup over sliced nectarines.
Above:
Plum tomatoes in a food mill.

Prick plums to prevent bursting when processed.

Preparing Syrups

Water	Sugar	Yield
4 cups	2 cups	5 cups light syrup
4 cups	3 cups	5½ cups medium syrup
4 cups	4¾ cups	6½ cups heavy syrup

Preparing Syrup for Fruits

Fresh fruit, except tomatoes, must be packed in a simple syrup of water and sugar or in fruit juice. Plain water is not recommended because it tends to leach out the fruit's natural flavor, sweetness, and color. For a lower calorie product, cover the fruit with fruit juice. Sliced Nectarines in Orange Juice on page 48 is an example. Without added sugar, however, the fruit's flavor and texture may suffer somewhat.

Syrup maintains the fruit's texture and shape, and points up its flavor. You can prepare syrup in a light, medium, or heavy sugar concentration to suit your taste.

To prepare syrup, combine the sugar and water in a saucepan, heat to boiling, and stir to dissolve the sugar. Keep the syrup hot until it's needed. If you wish to use honey, choose a mild clover honey that will not mask the fruit's natural flavor. Honey may be substituted for up to half the granulated sugar called for in the table below.

Brown sugar and molasses are not suitable for canning fruit because their flavor and color will overpower that of the fruit.

Plan on about 1/2 cup canning liquid for each pint jar and 3/4 to 1 cup for each quart jar.

Packing Methods

Fruits are packed raw or hot into jars. *Raw-packing* consists of placing food raw into canning jars and covering the food with hot liquid. This method is best for small, soft fruits that may become mushy and overcooked if cooked before being packed into jars and processed. *Hot-packing* involves bringing the food to a boil in syrup, juice, or water and cooking it briefly. The hot food is then packed into jars and the hot liquid poured over it. The hot-pack method is best for large, firm fruit such as apples and pears because these fruits shrink in cooking and become pliable so that you can fit more into a jar.

We prefer to raw-pack most fruit, including tomatoes, because this method retains the fruit's texture better than hot-packing. However, there is a tendency for some fruits, especially those packed in heavy syrup, to float to the top of the jar when the raw-pack method is used. This floating doesn't indicate spoilage, but it looks odd. The hot-pack method ensures that the jars will be well-filled because air and moisture are released from the food during cooking.

Most raw fruits can be packed fairly tightly into containers because the food will cook down during processing. Hot foods, however, must be packed firmly, but not so tightly that the produce is crushed. Overpacking containers may result in underprocessing. Leave about 1/2 inch of headspace at the top of each jar to allow for expansion of the contents during processing. Also, there should be enough packing liquid to surround and cover the food. Food at the top of the jar may darken if it is not covered with liquid.

The number of full jars you will get from a given quantity of fresh fruit depends on the quality, variety, maturity, and size of the fruit, and on the packing method used. For a general guide to yields, see page 9.

To peel fruit, dip in boiling water for 30 seconds. Plunge in cold water, then peel.

Step-by-Step Method for Canning Fruits and Tomatoes

1. *Prepare the jars.* Wash and rinse canning jars, lids, and rings. Keep jars hot—in a low oven (about 200°F) or in hot water—until they are ready to be used. This will prevent containers from breaking when filled with hot canning liquid. Scald rings and lids following the manufacturer's directions. Allow lids to remain in the water until you are ready to use them.

2. *Prepare the fruit.* Wash fruit and prepare it following the chart or recipe directions. Prepare only enough fruit for one canner load at a time. Make syrup, or heat fruit juice. Keep canning liquid hot until it's ready to be used.

3. *Fill the jars.*

   To raw-pack: Fill clean, hot jars with raw fruit. Halved fruit should be packed cavity side down; overlap pieces. Raw fruits can be packed fairly tightly because they will cook down during processing. Ladle hot liquid into jars to within 1/2 inch of the jar rim. **(Photos A and B.)**

   To hot-pack: Bring fruit to a boil in syrup or juice, or cook it briefly as the chart or recipe directs. Remove fruit from the syrup and pack into jars. Halved fruit should be packed cavity side down; overlap pieces. Ladle liquid into jars to within 1/2 inch of the jar rim. (There should be enough liquid to surround the fruit and cover it. Food at the top of the jar may darken if not covered with liquid.) **(Photos D, E, and F.)**

4. *Seal the jars.* Run a narrow spatula gently around the insides of the jars to release any bubbles. Add more liquid if necessary. Wipe jar rims clean, place lids on jars with sealing compound next to the glass, and screw on bands firmly, but not too tightly. **(Photo C.)**

5. *Process the jars.* Set jars on a rack in a water-bath canner or deep kettle filled with hot, but not boiling, water. Arrange jars on the rack so they do not touch each other or the sides of the kettle. Add hot water as needed to cover the jar tops with an inch or two of water. Cover the canner and quickly bring the water to a boil. Start counting the processing time when the water comes to a boil. Process the jars for the time given in the chart or recipe. At altitudes of about 3,000 feet, add 2 minutes' processing time for each additional 1,000 feet.

6. *Cool the jars.* Remove the jars from the kettle with a jar lifter immediately after processing. Cool the jars on a cooling rack or folded towel in a draft-free place. Leave space between the jars for air to circulate.

7. *Test for a seal.* Test the seal by pressing down the center of each lid with your finger. Lids that stay down are sealed; lids that pop back up are not. If a jar has not sealed by the time it is cool, refrigerate and eat the contents within a few days.

   Label and store jars in a clean, dark, dry place. Once opened, refrigerate the contents.

Guide to Canning Fruits and Tomatoes

Fruit	Quantity of Whole Fruit to Yield 1 Pint	Preparation	Processing Time* (minutes) Pint	Quart
Apples	1¼ to 1½ lb	Pare and core. Slice or quarter. Treat to prevent darkening. *Hot pack*: Cook slices or quarters 2 to 4 minutes in syrup or juice. Pack hot; cover with hot liquid. Seal.	15	15
Apricots	1 to 1¼ lb	Peel; leave whole, or halve and pit. Treat to prevent darkening. *Raw pack*: Fill jars with whole or halved fruit; cover with hot syrup or juice. Seal. *Hot pack*: Cook whole fruit in hot syrup 1 to 3 minutes. Pack hot; cover with hot liquid. Seal.	25 20	30 20
Berries (Strawberries are not recommended for canning.)	¾ to 1 lb	*Raw pack*: For raspberries or other soft berries, fill jar with raw fruit, shake down, and cover with hot liquid. Seal. *Hot pack*: For firm berries, add ½ cup sugar to 1 quart fruit in a pot. Cover pot, bring to a boil, and shake to prevent scorching and sticking. Pack hot, covered with their own juice. Seal.	10 10	15 10
Cherries	1 to 1½ lb	Prick skins and leave whole, or pit. *Raw pack*: Fill jars with cherries; cover with hot syrup or juice. Seal. *Hot pack*: For pitted cherries, follow directions for firm berries. For unpitted cherries, bring fruit to a boil in hot syrup or juice. Pack hot; cover with hot liquid. Seal.	20 10	25 10
Figs	¾ to 1¼ lb	*Hot pack*: Bring figs to a boil in syrup or juice; remove from heat and let stand 3 to 4 minutes. Pack hot, adding 1½ teaspoons lemon juice per pint. Cover with hot liquid. Seal.	90	90
Grapefruit	2 lb	Peel and remove white membrane. Section fruit over a bowl to catch the juice. Reserve 1 cup juice. *Raw pack*: Bring reserved juice and ½ cup sugar to a boil. Pack raw fruit into hot jars. Cover with hot liquid. Seal.	30	35
Grapes	2 lb	Remove stems. *Raw Pack*: Fill jars with grapes; cover with hot syrup or juice. Seal. *Hot pack*: Bring grapes to a boil in syrup or juice just to heat them through. Pack hot; cover with hot liquid. Seal.	20 15	20 15
Nectarines and Peaches	1 to 1½ lb	Peel, halve, and pit. Treat to prevent darkening. *Raw pack*: Fill jars with fruit halves, cavity side down. Cover with hot syrup or juice. Seal. *Hot pack*: Bring fruit to a boil in syrup or juice just to heat through. Pack hot; cover with hot liquid. Seal.	Freestone 20 / Clingstone 25 Freestone 15 / Clingstone 20	Freestone 25 / Clingstone 30 Freestone 20 / Clingstone 25
Pears	1 to 1½ lb	Pare, halve, and core. Pack as halves or slice. Treat to prevent darkening. (See page 43.) *Raw pack*: Fill jars with pear halves or slices. Cover with hot syrup or juice. Seal. *Hot pack*: Simmer pear halves or slices in syrup or juice 1 to 3 minutes. Pack hot; cover with hot liquid. Seal.	20 15	25 20
Pineapple	2 lb	Peel, core, and remove brown spots; cut fruit into chunks. *Hot pack*: Simmer pineapple in syrup or juice 5 minutes. Pack hot; cover with hot liquid. Seal.	15	20
Plums and Fresh Prunes	1 to 1½ lb	Leave whole and prick skins, or halve and pit. *Raw pack*: Fill jars with fruit; cover with hot syrup or juice. Seal. *Hot pack*: Bring fruit to a boil in hot syrup or juice just to heat through. Pack hot; cover with hot liquid. Seal.	15 20	15 20
Rhubarb	⅔ to 1 lb	Cut rhubarb into ½-inch lengths. To each quart of fruit, add ½ to 1 cup sugar. Mix and let stand 3 to 4 hours to extract juice. *Hot pack*: Bring fruit to a boil. Pack hot; cover with hot rhubarb juice. Seal.	10	10
Tomatoes	1¼ to 2¼ lb	Peel and core. *Raw pack*: Cut tomatoes in half, or leave whole. Pack in clean, hot jars. After 2 whole or 4 halves are packed, press down to repease juice. Press and cover tomatoes with as much of their own juice as possible. Add hot water, if necessary, to cover tomatoes, leaving ½-inch headspace. Add 1 teaspoon salt, 2 teaspoons vinegar or lemon juice, and fresh herbs, if desired, to each quart of tomatoes. Seal.	50	50

*At elevations higher than 3,000 feet, add 2 minutes' processing time for each additional 1,000 feet.

In less than two hours you can prepare Fruit Pie Filling from apples, peaches, or apricots.

FRUITS

Fruit Pie Filling

Use this pie filling for double-crust baked fruit pies, or spoon it straight from the jar into prebaked tartlet shells and decorate with whipped cream.

    10 pounds apricots, peaches, or apples

    1 cup plus 2 table-spoons quick-cooking tapioca

1-1/2 cups sugar

    3/4 cup lemon juice

    4 cups sugar

    Water

1. Peel, core or pit fruit, and slice. If you wish, treat to prevent darkening. (See page 43.)

2. In a mixing bowl combine tapioca, sugar, and lemon juice; reserve.

3. If prepared fruit was treated to prevent darkening, rinse well in cold water and drain. Place prepared fruit in a large pot with the sugar and enough water to prevent sticking and scorching. Heat to 190°F (just under boiling), stirring frequently.

4. Add reserved tapioca mixture and, stirring, reheat to 190°F. Do not boil.

5. Pour into clean, hot jars, leaving 1/2-inch headspace; seal.

6. Process in boiling-water bath 15 minutes.

Yield: About 6 quarts.

Chunky Applesauce

You'll love the chunky texture and fresh apple flavor. Add lemon juice or spices to make a spiced applesauce.

    20 large, tart, firm apples

    4 cups water

      White or brown sugar (to taste)

      Lemon juice or spices (optional)

1. Core and peel apples and remove any bruised spots. Treat for darkening. (See page 43.)

2. When all apples are prepared, remove from solution and rinse well with cold water. Quarter apples and place in large pot with the water. Simmer until apples are soft, stirring constantly.

3. Mash the apples in the pot until desired consistency is reached. Less mashing will produce a chunkier sauce.

4. Add sugar to taste. Lemon juice, spices (cloves, cinnamon, nutmeg), or brown sugar may be added if a spicy applesauce is desired. Stir well.

5. Return to a boil, stirring constantly.

6. Ladle into clean, hot jars, leaving 1/2-inch headspace; seal.

7. Process pint or quart jars in boiling-water bath 25 minutes.

Yield: About 4 pints.

Sliced Nectarines in Orange Juice

Canned in orange juice, these nectarines are lower in calories than those canned in syrup.

1-1/3 cups sugar

1 cup water

1/2 cup frozen orange juice concentrate, undiluted

1/4 cup lemon juice

4-1/4 to 4-1/2 pounds nectarines, peeled, pitted, and thinly sliced

1. Combine sugar, water, orange juice concentrate, and lemon juice in a large pot. Heat to boiling, stirring until sugar dissolves.

2. Add nectarines, bring back to a full boil, and boil for 2 minutes.

3. Pack fruit into clean, hot jars and fill with hot syrup, leaving 1/2-inch headspace. Run table knife or thin spatula gently between fruit and jar to release air bubbles; seal.

4. Process in boiling-water bath 20 minutes.

Yield: 5 pints.

Pears in Sherry

9 pounds fresh Bartlett pears

2-1/2 cups granulated sugar

1-1/3 cups water

1-1/3 cups golden sherry

1/2 cup lemon juice

1. Pare, halve, and core pears; treat to prevent darkening. (See page 43.)

2. Combine sugar, water, sherry, and lemon juice in large pot and heat to boiling.

3. Drain and rinse pears in cold water. Drain again and add to pot of syrup. Cover and cook until pears are almost tender (about 8 minutes).

4. Pack pears carefully in clean, hot jars. Fill jars with syrup, leaving 1/2-inch headspace. Run table knife or thin spatula gently between fruit and jar to release air bubbles. Seal.

5. Process in boiling-water bath 20 minutes.

Yield: 4 quarts.

Brandied Cherries

3-1/2 pounds Bing cherries

2 cups sugar

1-1/2 cups water

2 tablespoons lemon juice

1-1/4 cups California brandy

1. Rinse, stem, and pit cherries.

2. Combine sugar, water, and lemon juice in saucepan. Heat to a boil, stirring to dissolve sugar.

3. Pour 1/4 cup syrup into clean, hot jars. Fill jars with cherries.

4. Add 1/4 cup brandy and more syrup as necessary to fill each jar, leaving 1/2-inch headspace; seal.

5. Process in a boiling-water bath 20 minutes.

Yield: 5 pints.

Whole Cranberry Sauce

A traditional holiday favorite that can be enjoyed all year long. Make it before the holiday season so you'll have less to prepare the day before.

5 cups sugar

4 cups water

3 quarts (about 3 lb) cranberries

1. Boil sugar and water together in a 6-quart or larger pot for 5 minutes.

2. Add cranberries. Boil, without stirring, until skins burst.

3. Ladle boiling-hot mixture into clean, hot jars, leaving 1/2-inch headspace; seal.

4. Process in boiling-water bath 15 minutes.

Yield: About 6 pints.

Note: A spice bag containing a stick of cinnamon and/or a few whole cloves may be cooked with the sauce to give a spicy flavor. Remove spice bag before packing sauce in jars.

Orange shells make attractive holders for Whole Cranberry Sauce.

TOMATOES

Tomato Paste

The best tomato paste is made from Italian plum tomatoes, but any juicy, sweet variety will make an excellent product. Use tomato paste to add color to otherwise pallid dishes, and for thickening tomato sauces.

About 4 dozen large tomatoes

2 teaspoons salt (or more to taste)

1. Peel, core, and chop tomatoes. Measure; you should have 8 quarts. Add salt.

2. Place in large pot and simmer over low heat for about 1 hour. Stir often to prevent sticking.

3. Remove from heat and press through a fine sieve or put through food mill.

4. Return to kettle and continue to cook very slowly until paste holds its shape on a spoon (about 2 hours). Stir occasionally to prevent sticking.

5. Spoon into clean, hot jars, leaving 1/4-inch headspace; seal.

6. Process in boiling-water bath 30 minutes.

Yield: About 8 half-pints.

Marinara Sauce

This marinara sauce, mother of Italian red sauces, is best when made with vine-ripened Italian plum tomatoes.

1-1/4 cups onions, finely chopped

1-1/4 cups celery, finely chopped

1 cup carrots, finely chopped

1/2 cup olive oil

1 teaspoon minced garlic

8 pounds ripe tomatoes, peeled, seeded, and chopped

1 teaspoon sugar (optional)

Freshly ground black pepper

1 bay leaf

1 teaspoon dried basil, oregano, *or* marjoram

1/4 teaspoon fennel seed (optional)

1 teaspoon salt (or to taste)

1. Cook onion, celery, and carrots in the olive oil over medium heat in a large pot, covered, until the vegetables are tender (about 20 minutes). Stir occasionally.

2. Add garlic and cook 2 minutes.

3. Add tomatoes, sugar, and pepper. Simmer over low heat for 15 minutes.

4. Put the sauce through medium disc of a food mill.

5. Add remaining seasonings (except salt) and simmer, stirring often, until sauce reaches desired consistency (about 20 minutes). Add salt. Remove bay leaf.

6. Pack into clean, hot jars, leaving 1/2-inch headspace; seal.

7. Process in boiling-water bath 45 minutes.

Note: If you prefer a sauce with more texture, omit Step 4.

Use Seasoned Tomato Sauce as a base for Italian sauces on fresh linguini or spaghetti.

Seasoned Tomato Sauce

You'll never run out of ways to use tomato sauce made from juicy, vine-ripened tomatoes and seasoned with aromatic vegetables. It makes a fine base for a number of Italian sauces. When ready to use, add fresh herbs like basil or oregano, bay leaves, parsley, and garlic.

3 cups chopped onions (2 large)

2 cups sliced carrots (about 4 medium)

2 cups chopped celery

1-1/2 cups chopped green bell peppers (about 2 medium)

18 to 20 large tomatoes

1/4 cup olive oil

2 teaspoons salt (to taste)

1. Sauté onion, carrots, celery, and green peppers in olive oil until onions are limp and transparent.

2. Peel, core, and chop tomatoes; you should have 4 quarts. Add to vegetables and cook about 15 minutes.

3. Purée vegetables in a food processor, press through a fine sieve, or put through a food mill.

4. Add salt and cook sauce, uncovered, until thick (about 1 hour), stirring frequently to prevent sticking. (The final consistency should fall halfway between juice and paste).

5. Quickly ladle into clean, hot jars, leaving 1/4-inch headspace; seal.

6. Process in boiling-water bath 45 minutes.

Yield: About 4 to 5 pints.

How to Make Fruit Juices

Juices pressed from fresh, sun-ripened fruits evoke refreshing visions of summer when enjoyed on chilly winter mornings. Juices are made by extracting the liquid from fruit and sweetening it to taste. Sealed in canning jars, juices are acidic enough to require processing only in a water-bath canner.

Home-canned juices have many uses. They can be the base for syrups, dessert sauces, punches, sherbets, or fruit ices. Also, you can put up juice now and turn it into jelly later. If you sweeten the juice, note the amount of sugar added and subtract it from the amount called for in the jelly recipe. Turn the pulp left over from making juice into creamy fruit butters. (See page 39.)

An electric juice extractor is handy for extracting juice quickly from fruit, but juice can be extracted satisfactorily by hand. If you extract manually, you'll need a jelly bag and stand, or cheesecloth and a colander. You will want a large bowl to catch the juice when it drips through the jelly bag, and a large pot in which to heat the juice.

A

B

Step-by-Step Method for Making Juice

1. *Prepare the jars.* Wash and rinse canning jars and lids. Keep jars hot—in a low oven (about 200°F) or in hot water—until they are ready to be used. This will prevent jars from breaking when filled with hot juice. Scald rings and lids, following the manufacturer's directions. Allow lids to remain in the water until you use them.

2. *Prepare the fruit.* Wash fruit and prepare as recipe directs. Some fruits must be crushed or chopped and heated with water to render their juice. **(Photo A.)**

3. *Extract and strain the juice.* Follow recipe directions and extract juice as rapidly as possible with minimum exposure to air. Juice can be extracted by hand as follows. Line a colander with four thicknesses of damp, washed cheesecloth or clean muslin and place the colander over a bowl. Pour fruit and its juice into the cloth, and let juice drip into a large bowl. **(Photo B.)**

To use an electric juicer, follow manufacturer's directions.

4. *Heat and flavor the juice.* Heat the juice in a saucepan. If the juice needs sweetening, add sugar to taste and stir to dissolve it thoroughly. Blend juices for different flavor combinations, if desired.

5. *Fill the jars.* Fill clean, hot jars with hot juice, leaving 1/2-inch headspace. Wipe the jar rims clean, place lids on jars with the sealing compound next to the glass, and screw on the ring bands.

6. *Process the jars.* As each jar is filled, set it on a rack in a water-bath canner or deep kettle filled with hot, but not boiling, water. Arrange containers on the rack so they do not touch each other or the sides of the kettle. Add water as needed to cover the tops of the jars with an inch or two of water. Cover the canner and quickly bring the water to a boil. Begin timing the processing when the water comes to a boil. Process the jars as the recipe directs. At altitudes above 3,000 feet, add 2 minutes' processing time for each additional 1,000 feet.

7. *Cool the jars.* Remove the jars from the kettle immediately after processing. Cool the jars on a cooling rack or folded towel in a draft-free place. Leave space between the jars for air to circulate.

8. *Test for a seal.* Test the seal on jars by pressing down the center of each lid with your finger. Lids that stay down are sealed; lids that pop back up are not. If a jar has not sealed by the time it is cool, refreigerate and drink the juice within a few days.

Label and store juice in a cool, dark, dry place. The colder the storage temperature, the longer the juice will retain its fresh flavor, color, and vitamin content.

It takes less than an hour to prepare Tomato Juice. Fresh tomatoes are abundant in July.

3. Return juice to pot, stir in lemon juice to taste, and bring to a boil.

4. Quickly pour into clean, hot quart jars, leaving 1/2-inch headspace; seal.

5. Process in boiling-water bath 30 minutes.

Yield: 6 to 7 quarts.

Berry Juices

Any fresh, juicy berries can be used. Blackberries, boysenberries, loganberries, and raspberries make excellent juice.

Berries
Sugar

1. Place berries in a large pot, crush, and heat until berries are soft and render their juice.

2. Strain through jelly bag or a colander lined with four layers of cheesecloth into a large bowl. For a greater yield of juice, twist ends of bag or cheesecloth until most of the juice is extracted.

3. Measure and return juice to large pot; add 1 to 2 cups sugar to each gallon of juice (or to taste). Reheat to dissolve sugar.

4. Pour quickly into clean, hot jars, leaving 1/2-inch headspace; seal.

5. Process pints or quarts in boiling-water bath 15 minutes.

Note: If clearer juice is desired, before adding sugar let juice stand for 24 hours in refrigerator. Carefully ladle juice into pot (do not disturb sediment), add sugar, and proceed with Step 3.

JUICES

Tomato Juice

Firm, red-ripe tomatoes, cored and quartered

1/2 teaspoon salt to each quart of juice

1. Place tomatoes in a large pot and simmer until soft, stirring often.

2. Press through a fine sieve or put through a food mill to remove peels and seeds.

3. Measure juice and add salt. Reheat to boiling.

4. Pour immediately into clean, hot jars, leaving 1/2-inch headspace; seal.

5. Process in boiling-water bath: pints 10 minutes, quarts 15 minutes.

Vegetable Juice Cocktail

15 pounds ripe, red tomatoes, coarsely chopped (to measure about 8 qt)

1 large bell pepper, finely chopped

2 large onions, finely chopped

1-1/2 cups diced celery

2 bay leaves

12 fresh basil leaves (or 2 teaspoons dried basil)

1 tablespoon salt

2 teaspoons prepared horseradish

1/2 teaspoon freshly ground black pepper

3 tablespoons sugar (optional)

2 teaspoons Worcestershire sauce

1/2 cup lemon juice (or to taste)

1. Place measured tomatoes and all ingredients except lemon juice in a 12-quart or larger pot and simmer for about 30 minutes or until all the vegetables are soft. Remove basil leaves (if fresh basil is used).

2. Press vegetables through a fine sieve or put through a food mill to remove seeds, skins, and fibrous material.

In the fall when cranberries reach their peak, make Cranberry Juice to enjoy at holiday parties. Serve with clove-studded lemon slices and cookies.

bag again to extract remaining juice.

4. Place the two batches of juice in a large pot. Add sugar to suit your taste and 1 more quart water. Heat to dissolve sugar completely, but do not boil.

5. Quickly pour into clean, hot jars, leaving 1/2-inch headspace; seal.

6. Process in boiling-water bath 15 minutes.

Yield: 6 to 7 quarts.

Apple Juice

Apples

1. Quarter apples and use fruit press or cider mill to press out juice. Pour juice into a large pot and heat almost to the boil, but do not boil.

2. Skim off foam with a metal spoon and pour through a damp jelly bag or filter paper.

3. Quickly pour into clean, hot jars, leaving 1/2-inch headspace; seal.

4. Process in boiling-water bath 15 minutes.

Grape Juice

This method can be used for grapes or for berries and is the quickest way to can fresh juice.

Grapes (firm-ripe), washed, stemmed, halved, and seeded

Sugar

Water

1. Put 1 cup of grapes in the bottom of a clean, hot quart jar. Add 1/2 cup sugar.

2. Fill jar with boiling water, leaving 1/4-inch headspace; seal.

3. Process in a boiling-water bath 10 minutes.

Apricot Nectar

Nectars are most often made from fruits like apricots, pears, and peaches. They are fruit juices that are thickened with the finely sieved pulp of the fruit. This purée is thinned with ice water (to suit your taste) when served as a drink.

Apricots, pitted and sliced
Boiling water
Lemon juice (optional)
Sugar

1. Measure prepared fruit into a large pot and add 1 cup boiling water to each quart of fruit.

2. Simmer fruit in water until it is soft.

3. Press fruit and water

through a fine sieve or put through a food mill.

4. Measure the nectar into a large pot, add sugar to taste, and add 1 tablespoon lemon juice to each quart of nectar, if desired.

5. Reheat to dissolve sugar.

6. Pour into clean, hot jars, leaving 1/2-inch headspace; seal. Use half-pint or pint jars only.

7. Process in boiling-water bath 15 minutes.

Yield: 3-1/4 quarts prepared fruits and 3-1/4 cups water yield approximately 9 pints nectar.

Cranberry Juice

4 quarts (4 lb) cranberries
Water
3 to 3-1/2 cups sugar

1. Bring cranberries and 4 quarts water to a simmer in a large pot. (Do not boil.) Simmer 5 minutes, or until most berries burst.

2. Pour berries and juice into damp jelly bag or a colander lined with four layers of clean cheesecloth. Let juice drip into a large bowl. Do *not* squeeze the bag.

3. When you have extracted as much juice as possible from the pulp, return pulp to pot with 2 quarts water. Simmer 2 minutes. Pour this pulp and juice through jelly

Canned Fruits, Tomatoes and Juices Problem Solver

Problem	Cause	Prevention
Fruits darken after they are removed from jars	Fruits were not processed long enough to destroy enzymes.	1a. Process each fruit for the recommended length of time. Time is counted when water in the canner reaches a full boil. 1b. Boiling water in canner must cover the jar tops by 1 or 2 inches.
Pink, purple, blue, or red color in canned apples, pears, peaches, and quinces	A natural chemical change occurred in cooking the fruit. The food is still edible.	None.
Cloudy liquids (may indicate spoilage)	1. Minerals in water. 2. Spoilage.	1. Use soft water. 2. Process each fruit for the recommended length of time.
Canning liquid seeps out during processing	Jars filled too full.	Leave ½-inch headspace.
Jars seal, then unseal (spoilage—do not eat)	1. Food spoilage due to underprocessing. 2. Food particles left on the sealing surface. 3. Hairlike cracks or nicks in jar.	1. Process each fruit for the length of time specified. 2. Wipe rims and threads of jars before sealing. 3. Check jars; discard those unsuitable for canning.
Fruit darkens at top of jar	1. Cooking liquid did not cover fruit. 2. Too much headspace left in jar.	1. Fill jars with enough liquid to surround and cover fruit. 2. Fill jars, leaving ½-inch headspace.
Fruit floats	1. Jars filled too loosely. 2. Fruit syrup too heavy. 3. Overripe fruit.	1. Fill jars snugly with fruit, but do not overpack. 2. Try a medium or light syrup. 3. Can only perfectly ripe fruit.

Strawberry Lemonade

This is better than any pink lemonade you've ever tasted.

4 quarts strawberries, washed and hulled

4 cups lemon juice

3 quarts water

6 cups sugar

1. Purée strawberries in a blender, food processor, or food mill. For a clearer lemonade, extract juice from strawberries with a juice extractor.

2. Place strawberries in an 8-quart or larger pot. Add lemon juice, water, and sugar. Place mixture over medium heat and heat to 165°F, stirring occasionally. Do not boil.

3. Remove from heat and skim off foam with a metal spoon.

4. Quickly ladle hot juice into clean, hot jars, leaving 1/2-inch headspace; seal.

5. Process in boiling-water bath 15 minutes.

Yield: 6 to 7 quarts.

Combine ripe strawberries in late spring with fresh lemons to make Strawberry Lemonade.

Canning Vegetables, Meats, and Poultry

With this accurate, thorough guide you can confidently preserve the nutritious goodness of vegetables, meats, and poultry simply and safely. You'll also find special recipes that will add a zesty variety to your pantry collection.

Home-canning vegetables, meats, and poultry is a "centsible" practice when the food is really fresh and when it's processed within a few hours of purchase. The importance of freshness cannot be overemphasized. Vegetables, particularly, will rapidly lose their flavor, nutritional value, and keeping ability when left to stand between harvesting and processing.

The only safe way to can low-acid vegetables, meats, and poultry is in a steam pressure canner. Under steam pressure, these foods are processed for a specific length of time at 240°F, the temperature needed to inactivate and kill spoilage organisms present in low-acid foods. This high temperature is reached only under 10 pounds of pressure at sea level.

Altitude is an important factor in talking about pressure. As the altitude increases, the temperature at which food boils decreases. Therefore, at altitudes above sea level, you must make

Jars of fresh peas are ready to be covered with liquid, capped tightly, and processed for 40 minutes in a steam pressure canner.

adjustments in pressure to ensure that foods are adequately processed. The processing times and pressures for the charts and recipes in this chapter are based on altitudes up to 2,000 feet. If you live at a higher elevation, use the table below to adjust the pressure.

When using a pressure canner with a weighted gauge at an altitude above 2,000 feet, process at 15 pounds of pressure.

The essential piece of equipment needed to can low-acid foods is a steam pressure canner, described and illustrated on page 14. Do not substitute a pressure cooker or a pressure saucepan; their purpose is fast cooking. You'll also need a 6-quart or larger pot to pre-

pare food for canning, and standard canning jars. Measuring utensils, knives, a narrow metal spatula, a slotted spoon, a wide-mouth funnel, a jar lifter, tongs, and a timer also come in handy.

The charts on pages 58 and 59 give directions for canning a variety of vegetables, meats, and poultry. The recipes that follow are delicious examples of home-canned foods sure to outshine their store-bought counterparts. They're real money-savers, too.

Before you start, read Chapter 2, "A Short Course on Canning," starting on page 13.

If you have any difficulties along the way, refer to the Problem Solver chart on page 63.

Altitude Chart

Altitude Above Sea Level	Process At
2,000 to 3,000 feet	11½ pounds
3,000 to 4,000 feet	12 pounds
4,000 to 5,000 feet	12½ pounds
5,000 to 6,000 feet	13 pounds
6,000 to 7,000 feet	13½ pounds
7,000 to 8,000 feet	14 pounds
8,000 to 9,000 feet	14½ pounds
9,000 to 10,000 feet	15 pounds

Detecting Food Spoilage

As long as you follow the instructions precisely for preparing and processing vegetables, meats, and poultry, there is little or no chance of food spoilage. However, botulism, a fatal form of food poisoning, can occur when low-acid foods are not canned by the steam pressure method or when they're canned incorrectly.

Chapter 1 discussed food spoilage and its causes in detail. Listed here are a few pointers for detecting spoilage in low-acid foods. Inspect each jar carefully before serving the canned food. Underprocessed foods will foster the growth of botulism spores and other harmful microorganisms that grow in an airtight environment. Leakage from jars, bulging lids, upward-moving bubbles, patches of mold, and a foamy or murky appearance are visible signs that a product is not edible. A pleasant odor characteristic of the food canned is a good sign of properly preserved food. Use your eyes, nose, and good sense to detect spoilage. If a food doesn't look or smell right, *don't eat it.* Don't even taste it. Botulism can't be seen or smelled; therefore, vegetables, meats, and poultry that have been incorrectly handled may not show signs of spoilage. To be on the safe side, the U.S. Department of Agriculture strongly recommends that you *boil* all low-acid foods in a covered saucepan for at least 10 minutes before tasting or serving them. If the food appears to be spoiled or develops an off-odor, discard it. Don't try to salvage the food—it isn't worth the worry.

When you detect food spoilage from low-acid foods, immediately dump the jar, its closures, and contents into a pan of strong detergent solution. Boil for 30 minutes. Then flush the food and liquid down the toilet and discard the jars and lids. Wash your hands and anything else that might have come in contact with the contaminated food in a bleach solution (4 parts water to 1 part bleach).

Canning Vegetables

Vegetables are at their flavorful best when they're picked young and tender. Big, overmature vegetables will result in canned goods that are tough and flavorless. Remember, good flavor depends both on early picking and on processing very

shortly after picking. (See Chapter 1, page 6, for more about where to obtain fresh vegetables.) Store vegetables in the refrigerator until you process them.

Vegetables are packed either hot or raw into jars. *Hot-packing* involves cooking the vegetables in a small amount of water. The hot food is then packed into hot jars and the cooking liquid is poured over it. This method is best for crisp vegetables—cooking makes the vegetables tender and pliable so that you can fit more in a jar. *Raw-packing* consists of packing raw vegetables into jars and covering them with hot water. This method is not as common for vegetables as it is for fruits, but it is a satisfactory way to can small vegetables and pieces. When the chart on page 55 gives instructions for both raw- and hot-packing, the choice is yours.

Salt added to vegetables in canning is merely for seasoning, so it's optional. Use of a salt substitute is not recommended because it leaves an aftertaste. Instead, add the salt substitute when vegetables are heated just before serving.

Step-by-Step Method for Canning Vegetables

This method demonstrates using a steam pressure canner with a weighted gauge. Use this step-by-step instruction as a guide. Refer to the instruction manual that accompanies your pressure canner for specific directions.

1. *Prepare the jars, lids, and ringbands and the pressure canner.* Wash and rinse canning jars and closures. Keep jars hot—in a low (200°F) oven or in hot water—until they are ready to be used. This will prevent containers from breaking when filled with hot canning liquid. Scald lids and rings following manufacturer's directions. Allow lids to remain in the water until you are ready to use them.

Place the pressure canner on a heating element, insert the rack, and pour in hot tap water to a depth of 2 to 3 inches. Cover the canner (do not fasten the lid), and bring the water to a boil. Keep the water hot while you prepare the vegetables. **(Photo A.)**

2. *Prepare the vegetables.* Working quickly, wash and sort vegetables according to size; can those of uniform size together to ensure even processing. Prepare vegetables for cooking following the chart or recipe directions. Prepare only enough vegetables to fill one canner load at a time. **(Photo B.)**

3. *Fill the jars.*
   To cold-pack: Fill clean, hot jars with raw vegetables.

D

F

E

G

H

Do not pack the jars too tightly. Pour boiling water into the jars, leaving adequate headspace as the chart or recipe indicates. **(Photo C.)**

To hot-pack: Cook vegetables in water as the chart or recipe directs. Save the cooking liquid. Fill clean, hot jars with hot vegetables. Do not pack the jars too tightly. Bring the cooking liquid back to a boil and pour it into the jars, dividing the liquid evenly among them. Add boiling water as necessary to fill the jars to the point indicated in the chart or recipe. **(Photo D.)**

4. *Seal the jars.* Run a narrow spatula gently around the inside of the jars to release any air bubbles. Add more liquid if necessary. Wipe jar rims clean, place lids on jars with sealing compound next to the glass, then screw on the ring bands firmly, but not too tightly. As each jar is sealed, place it in the pressure canner to keep the food hot. **(Photo E.)**

5. *Process the jars.* Place jars on a rack in the canner. Arrange them so they do not touch each other or the sides of the kettle. Following the canner instructions, fasten the canner lid securely. Exhaust the canner by opening the petcock (pressure regulator) and letting air escape through the vent pipe for 10 minutes (or following canner manual instructions). (Air left in the canner would prevent the temperature from rising as high as is necessary.) **(Photo F.)**

After venting, close the petcock (pressure regulator) and bring the canner to 10 pounds of pressure—240°F. **(Photo G.)** Make altitude adjustments if necessary. (See page 55.) Start timing the process when the pressure level is reached. Process the jars for the length of time given in the chart or recipe. Regulate the heating element when necessary. Do not lower the pressure by opening the petcock. Watch pressure carefully—fluctuating pressure draws liquids out of the jars, resulting in a poor seal.

6. *Cool the canner.* Turn off the heat and let canner cool undisturbed. This will take about 30 minutes. Never try to speed this process. Then slowly open the petcock (pressure regulator). Allow the canner to cool an additional 15 minutes, then remove the lid. Open it away from you to avoid a steam burn. **(Photo H.)**

7. *Cool the jars.* Leave the jars in the canner 15 minutes or more—do not disturb the seal. Then remove the jars with a jar lifter and set them on a cooling rack or folded towel in a draft-free place. Leave space between the jars for air to circulate.

8. *Test the seal.* After the jars have cooled completely, test for a seal by pressing down the center of each lid with your finger. Lids that stay down are sealed. Jars that do not seal must be refrigerated and the contents eaten within a few days.

Remove the ring bands if desired. Label and store the jars in a cool, dark, dry place.

Guide to Canning Vegetables

Vegetables*	Approximate Quantity of Whole Vegetables to Yield 1 Quart	Preparation		
Asparagus	3 to 4½ lb	Remove scales, break off woody ends, and cut stalks into lengths ¾ inch shorter than the jar height, or into 1- to 2-inch pieces. Cook asparagus 1 to 3 minutes in boiling water, then plunge into cold water. Pack stalks (not too tightly) with cut ends down or fill with cut pieces to within 1 inch of jar rims. Add salt—½ teaspoon for pint jars; 1 teaspoon for quarts. Add boiling cooking liquid to cover asparagus, leaving ½-inch headspace. Seal.	28	32
Beans, green	1½ to 2½ lb	Trim beans and string beans if necessary. Leave whole or cut into 1- to 2-inch pieces.		
		Hot pack: Boil beans 2 to 5 minutes until pliable. Pack hot into hot jars up to shoulder of jar. Add salt—½ teaspoon for pint jars; 1 teaspoon for quarts. Add boiling cooking liquid to cover beans, leaving ¾-inch headspace. Seal.	25	30
		Cold pack: Omit precooking and proceed as above.	20	25
Beans, lima	3 to 5 lb (in pods)	Hull beans. Boil beans 1 to 4 minutes until skins wrinkle. Pack hot beans loosely into hot jars to within 1 inch of pint jar tops; 1½ inches for quarts. Add salt—½ teaspoon for pint jars; 1 teaspoon for quarts. Add boiling cooking liquid or water to cover beans, leaving 1-inch headspace. Seal.	40	50
Beets	2½ to 3½ lb	Scrub beets. Leave roots and 1 inch of tops. Boil for 15 minutes. Plunge into cold water; peel, trim, and slice ¼ inch thick. Reheat beets in a small amount of water. Pack hot beets into hot jar, filling jars to the shoulder. Add salt—½ teaspoon to pint jars; 1 teaspoon to quarts. Add boiling liquid in which beets were reheated and add additional water if necessary, leaving ½-inch headspace. Seal.	35	40
Carrots	2½ to 3 lb	Scrape and slice carrots, or cut into sticks 1 inch shorter than the jar height.		
		Hot pack: Bring carrots to a boil in water to cover. Pack hot slices into hot jars up to the shoulder; or arrange sticks upright to within 1 inch of the tops. Add salt—½ teaspoon for pint jars; 1 teaspoon for quarts. Add boiling cooking liquid to cover carrots, leaving ¾-inch headspace. Seal.	30	30
		Cold pack: Omit precooking and pack as directed above. Seal.	30	30
Celery	1½ to 2½ lb	Remove leafy tops and coarse strings. Slice, or cut celery into sticks 1 inch shorter than the jar height.		
		Hot pack: Cook celery sticks 1 to 3 minutes until tender-crisp. Pack hot celery into hot jars up to the shoulder. Add salt—½ teaspoon for pint jars; 1 teaspoon for quarts. Add boiling cooking liquid or water, leaving ½-inch headspace. Seal.	35	35
		Cold pack: Arrange sticks upright or pack slices loosely to jar shoulder. Proceed as above.	30	30
Corn	4 to 6 lb (in husks) (6 to 8 ears)	Remove husks and silk.		
		Whole kernel corn: Cut kernels from corn ⅔ deep. Do not scrape cobs. To each 4 cups of corn, add 2 cups boiling water. Bring to a boil over medium heat. Pack hot corn and liquid into hot jars, leaving 1-inch headspace. Add ½ teaspoon salt for pint jars; 1 teaspoon for quarts. Seal.	55	75
		Cream-style corn: Cut corn from cob halfway through the kernels, then scrape the milky juice left on the cob in with the cut corn. (This is the "cream.") To each 4 cups of cream-corn mixture add 2 cups boiling water. Heat to boiling, stirring over medium heat. Fill hot *pint* jars with boiling corn and liquid, leaving 1-inch headspace. Add ½ teaspoon salt to each pint. Seal. (Do not pack in quart jars; the mixture is too dense.)	85	—

Vegetables*	Approximate Quantity of Whole Vegetables to Yield 1 Quart	Preparation	Processing Time* (minutes)	
			Pint	Quart
Mushrooms	1½ lb	Trim stems and soak mushrooms in cold water 10 minutes. Wipe clean. Leave small mushrooms whole; halve or quarter larger ones. Steam mushrooms over boiling water 4 minutes. Pack hot into hot *pint* jars to the jar shoulder. (Do not pack in quart jars.) Add ½ teaspoon salt to each pint. Add boiling water to cover mushrooms, leaving ½-inch headspace. Seal.	30	—
Peas, green	3 to 5 lb	Shell young, tender peas.		
		Cold pack: Pack peas loosely to within 1 inch of jar tops. Add salt—½ teaspoon for pint jars; 1 teaspoon for quarts. Cover with boiling water, leaving 1½-inch headspace. (Water will be below top of peas.) Seal.	40	45
		Hot pack: Bring peas to a boil in water to cover. Pack hot peas loosely into hot jars to within ¼ inch of tops. Add salt—½ teaspoon for pint jars; 1 teaspoon for quarts. Cover with boiling cooking liquid or water, leaving 1-inch headspace. (Water will be below top of peas.) Seal.	40	45
Peppers, bell	2 to 3 lb	Remove stem and seeds. Place in a 400°F oven until skins are slightly scorched and separate from flesh. Plunge into cold water and peel. Cut into large slices or chunks. Pack into hot jars, leaving 1-inch headspace. Add ½ teaspoon salt and 1 tablespoon lemon juice or vinegar to pint jars; 1 teaspoon salt and 2 tablespoons lemon juice or vinegar to quarts. Cover with boiling water, leaving ½-inch headspace. Seal.	35	40
Potatoes, new (Other varieties are not recommended for canning.)	3 to 4 lb	Peel new potatoes. Leave small ones whole; halve larger ones.		
		Cold pack: Pack raw into jars to jar shoulder. Pour a boiling brine made by adding 1½ teaspoons salt to each quart water over potatoes, leaving 1-inch headspace. Seal.	35	40
		Hot pack: Boil potatoes 10 minutes. Proceed as directed above. Seal.	35	40
Spinach	2 to 3 lb	Steam spinach leaves until wilted. Fill hot jars with spinach, leaving ½-inch headspace. Add salt— ¼ teaspoon for pint jars; ½ teaspoon for quarts. Add boiling water, leaving ½-inch headspace. Seal.	70	90
Sweet potatoes (packed in syrup)	2½ to 3 lb	Boil sweet potatoes about 20 minutes; remove skins. Cut into medium-size pieces. While potatoes cook, prepare a medium sugar syrup (page 44.) Pack potatoes hot into jars, leaving 1-inch headspace. Fill to within ½ inch of the top with boiling syrup. Seal.	60	95
Summer squash: crookneck zucchini patty pan	2 to 2½ lb	Trim ends; do not peel. Cut into ½-inch-thick slices.		
		Hot pack: Bring squash just to a boil in a small amount of liquid. Pack hot into hot jars, filling loosely to jar shoulder. Add salt—½ teaspoon for pint jars; 1 teaspoon for quarts. Cover with boiling cooking liquid, leaving ½-inch headspace. Seal.	30	40
		Cold pack: Pack slices tightly into jars to within 1 inch of tops. Add salt—½ teaspoon for pint jars; 1 teaspoon for quarts. Cover with boiling cooking liquid, leaving ½-inch headspace. Seal.	25	30
Tomatoes		See Guide to Canning Fruits, page 46.		
Winter squash: banana butternut Hubbard pumpkin	2 to 3 lb	Cut squash into large chunks, scraping away all fibrous material and seeds. Boil in a small amount of water until tender. Scrape meat from rind and mash or pur§ee. Add salt—½ teaspoon for pint jars; 1 teaspoon for quarts. Bring to a boil. Pack hot into hot jars to within ¾ inch of tops. Seal.	85	115

*Strongly flavored vegetables such as broccoli, brussels sprouts, cabbage, cauliflower, and rutabagas discolor and their flavor grows even stronger when canned.

VEGETABLES

Tomato Soup

4 quarts peeled, cored, chopped tomatoes (about 2 dozen large)

3 cups chopped onions

2 cups chopped celery

2 cups chopped red bell peppers (about 4 medium)

1-1/2 cups sliced carrots (about 3 medium)

2 teaspoons salt

1 teaspoon dried basil (or 2 teaspoons fresh, chopped basil)

1 bay leaf

1. In a large pot, cook tomatoes until soft; press through a sieve or put through a food mill.

2. Meanwhile, in a saucepan, combine onions, celery, peppers, and carrots with enough water to cover; cook until all vegetables are tender. Drain. Put vegetables through food mill or press through fine sieve.

3. Combine tomato and vegetable purées in a large pot; add salt and herbs. Cook slowly until thick, about 1 hour, stirring frequently to prevent sticking. Remove bay leaf.

4. Pour into clean, hot pint jars, leaving 1/2-inch headspace; seal.

5. Process in pressure canner 20 minutes at 10 pounds pressure for altitudes up to 2,000 feet. (See chart, page 55, for higher altitudes.)

Yield: About 6 pints.

Split Pea Soup

1 pound split peas

3 cups water

6 cups chicken broth

3 slices thick bacon, chopped

1/2 cup chopped onion

1 cup diced celery

1 cup diced carrots

1/2 teaspoon dry mustard

1/4 teaspoon coarsely ground pepper

1 teaspoon salt, or to taste

1/4 teaspoon dried oregano, crumbled

1 cup diced ham

1. Combine all ingredients except oregano and ham and simmer, covered, 2 hours or until peas are tender. Add oregano and ham and simmer 30 minutes more.

2. Ladle soup into clean, hot jars, leaving 1-inch headspace; seal.

3. Process in a pressure canner at 10 pounds pressure: 50 minutes for pints; 1 hour for quarts.

Yield: 6 to 7 pints or 3 quarts.

Bacon, ham, and fresh peas give Split Pea Soup a hearty taste. Serve with bread sticks or warm biscuits.

Herbed Green Beans

4 pounds green beans, trimmed and cut in 1-inch pieces (about 16 cups)

2 cups chopped onions

1-1/3 cups chopped celery

2 cloves garlic, minced

1/2 teaspoon dried rosemary, crushed

1/2 teaspoon dried basil, crushed

Salt

1. Bring a large pot of water to a boil. Cook beans in boiling water 2 to 4 minutes. Drain beans, reserving cooking liquid.

2. Combine beans, onions, celery, garlic, rosemary, and basil.

3. Pack into clean, hot jars, leaving 3/4-inch headspace. Bring reserved liquid to a boil. Fill jars with boiling liquid, leaving 3/4-inch headspace. Add 1/2 teaspoon salt per pint or 1 teaspoon salt per quart. Seal.

4. Process in pressure canner: pints 25 minutes, quarts 30 minutes at 10 pounds pressure for altitudes up to 2,000 feet. (See chart, page 55, for higher altitudes.)

Yield: 8 pints or 4 quarts.

Boston Baked Beans

1 quart (about 2 lb) dried navy beans

1/2 pound salt pork, cut in small pieces

3 small onions, sliced

2/3 cup brown sugar, packed

2 teaspoons salt

2 teaspoons Dijon-style or dry mustard

2/3 cup molasses

1. Wash beans in cold water. Place in large pot; cover with cold water, bring to a boil, and allow to stand 1 hour. Drain. Cover with fresh water and simmer until tender (about 1 hour).

2. Drain beans and measure 4 cups cooking liquid. Place beans, cooking liquid, and remaining ingredients in a baking dish or casserole; mix well. Bake in 350°F oven for 1-1/2 hours.

3. Pack into clean, hot jars, leaving 1-inch headspace; seal.

4. Process in pressure canner: pints 1 hour, 20 minutes; quarts 1 hour, 35 minutes at 10 pounds pressure for altitudes up to 2,000 feet. (See chart, page 55, for higher altitudes.)

Yield: 6 to 7 pints; 3 quarts.

Note: Beans should be "soupy" when packed in jars.

Canning Meats and Poultry

Wouldn't it be fun to put up jars of homemade mincemeat for use in holiday baked goods or to give as gifts? Or how convenient to be able to take a jar of homemade beef or chicken stock off the pantry shelf to use as a base for soups and stews. These recipes and many more may be canned at home the same way vegetables are—by the steam pressure method. To prepare the recipes in this section, simply follow the step-by-step method for packing and processing vegetables outlined on page 56.

Freezing is the fastest and easiest method of preserving meat. Not everyone has a freezer big enough to store large quantities, however, and in some areas power failures are a problem, so canning may be the answer.

Meats that can well are beef, veal, lamb, and pork; good poultry choices include chicken, turkey, and game birds. If you raise your own animals, we suggest you have them slaughtered and butchered at a commercial establishment—they will handle the meat under the sanitary conditions and controlled temperatures required by government regulations for commercial butchering.

To can meats and poultry, prepare and pack them as directed in the chart below, and then process them following the procedure outlined for vegetables.

Fish and seafood require faultless handling and their preparation must be very carefully executed. We suggest that you contact your local county extension service for advice and instructions. Pickling seafood, however, is easy and safe, and several delicious recipes are given in Chapter 7 (page 86).

Guide to Canning Meats and Poultry

Food	Preparation	Processing Time (minutes)	
		Pints	Quarts
Meats: Beef Pork Lamb Veal	Cut meat from bone; trim off fat. Cut meat into thick strips or chunks to fit jars. Place meat in a large pan and add a small amount of water, just enough to keep meat from sticking. Cover and cook slowly until the meat is medium done. Pack hot meat loosely into hot jars, leaving 1-inch headspace. Add salt—½ teaspoon for pint jars; 1 teaspoon for quarts. Cover meat with boiling meat juice, extended with boiling water as necessary, leaving 1-inch headspace. Seal.	75	90
Poultry (This method also is suitable for canning rabbit and wild fowl.)	Debone breast; cut off boney ends of drumsticks, leaving meaty portion. Trim fat. *Hot pack with bone:* In a pan, cover raw poultry with boiling water. Cover pan and cook until medium done. Pack hot meat loosely into hot jars, leaving 1-inch headspace. Place drumsticks and thighs with skin side next to the glass. Fit breast and small pieces into the center. Cover poultry with cooking liquid, leaving 1-inch headspace. Add salt—½ teaspoon for pint jars; 1 teaspoon for quarts. Seal.	65	75
	Hot pack without bone: Bone poultry, leaving the skin on. Proceed as directed above.	75	90

Use Old-Fashioned Mincemeat in pies, tarts, or cookies. Serve with whipped cream or ice cream.

MEATS AND POULTRY

Beef Stock

Soups, stews, and sauces are always better when made with homemade stock. You'll never buy the commercially canned product again once you've made your own.

1/4 cup oil

2 pounds stewing beef, cubed

4 quarts meaty beef bones, cut in 1-inch lengths

5 quarts water

2 to 4 teaspoons salt (to taste)

12 black peppercorns

2 bay leaves

1/2 teaspoon dried thyme (or several sprigs fresh thyme)

10 sprigs parsley

2 onions, quartered

5 carrots, peeled and cut

4 stalks celery, cut up

1. Place oil in a large, heavy skillet and brown beef and bones on all sides over medium heat. (Beef bones and beef can also be browned in the oven in a roasting pan. Roast at 375°F for about 1 hour, turning occasionally.)

2. When beef is brown, pour a little water into the pan and scrape up the pan juices. Pour contents of skillet into a 12-quart or larger stockpot.

3. Cover beef and bones with the water and bring to a boil. Skim off foam that rises to top. Add remaining ingredients and add more water if necessary to cover. Reduce heat and simmer for 5 to 6 hours. Continue to skim when necessary.

4. Strain stock through cheesecloth-lined colander or wire-mesh sieve into a large pot. Skim off fat (see note) and taste for seasoning. Return to boil.

5. Quickly pour into clean, hot pint jars, leaving 1/2-inch headspace; seal.

6. Process in pressure canner 45 minutes at 10 pounds pressure for altitudes up to 2,000 feet. (See chart, page 55, for higher altitudes.)

Yield: About 8 pints.

Note: The best way to remove fat from stock is to cool stock, refrigerate for several hours, and remove all solidified fat from top.

Chicken Stock

5 pounds chicken parts (including backs, necks, wings, gizzards, and bones)

4 quarts cold water

2 onions, peeled and quartered

2 carrots, chopped

2 celery stalks, chopped

10 peppercorns

4 sprigs parsley

2 bay leaves

1/2 teaspoon dried thyme (or several sprigs fresh thyme)

2 cloves garlic (optional)

2 cloves (optional)

Salt (to taste)

1. Place chicken parts (do not use livers) in a large stockpot, cover with the water, and bring to a boil. Skim off foam as it rises to the surface.

2. Reduce heat, add remaining ingredients, and simmer for 3 to 4 hours. Skim as necessary.

3. Strain stock through cheesecloth-lined colander or wire-mesh sieve. Skim fat from surface (see note) and taste for seasoning. Add salt if necessary. Return to boil.

4. Pour hot stock into clean, hot pint jars, leaving 1-inch headspace; seal.

5. Process in pressure canner 45 minutes at 10 pounds pressure for altitudes up to 2,000 feet. (See chart, page 55, for higher altitudes.)

Yield: About 8 pints.

Note: The best way to remove fat from stock is to cool stock, refrigerate for several hours, and remove all solidified fat from top.

Old-Fashioned Mincemeat

5 cups (about 2 lb) lean beef, cooked and finely chopped (by hand or using a food chopper)

1 quart (about 1 lb) ground suet

3 quarts (about 12 medium) tart apples, pared, cored, and finely chopped

2 large oranges, peeled, seeded, and finely chopped (about 1-1/2 cups)

1/3 cup finely chopped orange peel (2 oranges)

1/4 cup lemon juice

2 pounds (about three 11-oz packages) currants

3 pounds raisins (half golden, half dark)

1/2 pound candied citron, chopped

4-2/3 cups (2 lb) packed dark brown sugar

1 tablespoon *each* salt, cinnamon, and allspice

2 teaspoons nutmeg

1 teaspoon cloves

1/4 teaspoon ginger

1 quart sweet cider or apple juice (or 3 cups juice and 1 cup brandy)

1. Mix together all ingredients (except brandy) in a large pot; simmer 1 hour, stirring occasionally to prevent sticking. Remove from heat and stir in brandy (optional).

2. Pack into clean, hot pint or quart jars, leaving 1-inch headspace; seal.

3. Process pints or quarts in pressure canner 20 minutes at 10 pounds pressure at altitudes below 2,000 feet. (See chart, page 55, for higher altitudes.)

Yield: About 14 pints or 7 quarts.

Chili Con Carne

1 pound pinto or red beans

4 pounds stewing beef, cut in 1/2-inch cubes

4 tablespoons oil

3 cups water

1-1/2 cups chopped onions

2 cloves garlic, minced

4 cups peeled, seeded, chopped tomatoes and their juice (or use canned tomatoes)

2-1/2 to 3 teaspoons salt

1 tablespoon chili powder

2 teaspoons dried oregano

1/2 teaspoon ground cumin

1/2 teaspoon dried hot red pepper flakes

1. Wash beans, cover with cold water, and soak overnight (or cover with water, bring to a boil, remove from heat, and let stand for 1 hour). Drain beans and set aside.

2. In a large skillet, brown beef in oil. Place meat in a 4-quart or larger pot with beans and remaining ingredients and the 3 cups of water. Bring to a boil. Reduce heat and simmer, covered, for 1-1/2 hours, stirring occasionally. Add more liquid when necessary to keep beans from sticking. Taste for seasoning.

3. Pack chili into clean, hot jars, leaving 1-inch headspace; seal.

4. Process in pressure canner: pints 1-1/4 hours, quarts 1-1/2 hours at 10 pounds pressure for altitudes up to 2,000 feet. (See chart, page 55, for higher altitudes.)

Yield: 6 pints or 3 quarts.

Canned Vegetables, Meats and Poultry Problem Solver

Problem	Cause	Prevention
Green vegetables lose their bright green color	Heat breaks down chlorophyll, the green coloring in plants.	None.
Green vegetables turn brown	1. Vegetables were overcooked.	1. Time cooking and processing exactly. Vegetables are still edible.
	2. Vegetables were too mature for canning.	2. Can young, tender vegetables at their peak of freshness.
	3. Vegetables were not completely covered with liquid.	3. Cover and surround vegetables with cooking liquid or water.
White sediment on bottoms of jars	1. Fallout of starch in vegetables (corn, peas, lima beans).	1. None.
	2. Minerals in water.	2. Use soft water.
	3. Bacterial spoilage. (Liquid is murky and food soft—do not eat.)	3. Process each vegetable by the steam pressure method and for the specified length of time.
White crystals in canned spinach	Calcium and oxalic acid in the spinach combine to form white crystals	None.
Cloudy liquids (may indicate spoilage)	1. Minerals in water.	1. Use soft water.
	2. Starch in vegetables.	2. None.
	3. Spoilage. Do not use.	3. Process each food by the steam pressure method and for the length of time specified.
Jars seal, then unseal (spoilage—do not eat)	1. Food spoilage due to underprocessing.	1. Process each food for the length of time specified.
	2. Food particles left on the sealing surface.	2. Wipe rims and threads of jars before sealing.
	3. Hairlike cracks or nicks in jar.	3. Check jars; discard those unsuitable for canning.
Canning liquid seeps out during processing.	Jars filled too full.	Leave adequate headspace as directed in chart or recipes.

All About Pickling

The "how to" of fermentation pickling as well as the time-saving fresh-pack method, and a fine collection of recipes for all-American favorites and international specialities.

To many, a pickle means the traditional cucumber preserved in vinegar or brine, flavored with dill, and put up in jars. But a pickle is any vegetable, fruit, meat, or combination preserved with vinegar and/or salt. Pickles may be sweetened, peppered, dilled, spiced, soured, or sauced. And although most pickled foods are eventually canned, some may be simply marinated and refrigerated.

Pickling Terms

Almost anything you eat may be pickled. *Vegetable pickles*, which include the all-time favorite cucumber, are either fresh-packed by a quick brining process or fermented for longer periods. *Fruit pickles* are made from fresh fruit simmered in a spicy sweet-sour syrup. *Pickled meats or seafood* are usually simply marinated for short periods and refrigerated. *Relishes* are piquant blends of chopped or ground vegetables and/or fruits, spices, and vinegar. Relishes may be hot, spicy, sweet, or sour, depending on the recipe. *Chutneys* are a

With the addition of vinegar these cucumbers and flavorings will become delicious Dill Spear Pickles (recipe page 69).

type of relish prepared from chopped fruits and/or vegetables, nuts, and spices. Many East Indian foods are complemented by chutneys, but they can be served as a condiment with many other foods.

A substance often used in pickling is *brine*. Simply put, brine is salt dissolved in liquid. It can be made in two ways. Salt can be dissolved in vinegar and water. The brine is then heated, poured over the food packed in jars, and the jars sealed. Brine also results from salting animal or plant tissue. The salt draws the moisture from the tissue and combines with the juices to create a brine. Sauerkraut is an example.

Stocking the Kitchen

Pickling requires little specialized equipment—anyone who has canned will have it all. And the average kitchen larder will have all but a small percentage of the ingredients necessary to get you started.

Recipes for quick, fresh-pack pickles require containers in which to marinate and cook the ingredients. Use enameled, stainless steel, or glass cookware. Iron, copper, or aluminum may react chemically with the acid and salt in the pickling mixture, discoloring the

food and imparting a metallic flavor. Never use galvanized (zinc) cookware when pickling. The chemical combination is downright dangerous. The fermentation method usually involves large quantities; therefore, stone crocks or large glass containers are needed.

Proper tools make pickling easy and safe. You'll need measuring utensils, long-handled spoons, a vegetable peeler, a ladle, a skimmer, sharp knives, a colander, a timer, and a cooling rack. You also may need a vegetable brush to clean produce, a wide-mouth funnel to fill jars easily, a jar lifter to lift hot jars from boiling water, a

kitchen scale, and cheesecloth or muslin to make spice bags. Particular techniques may require more specialized equipment such as a food mill or a food grinder (often called a meat grinder).

You'll also need canning jars for putting up pickled products and a water-bath canner for processing them. This is the same equipment required for canning and it's described in detail on page 13.

Pickling cucumbers have the shape, texture (especially spiny skin), and flavor that make them good for canning.

Fresh, ripe produce, vinegar, sugar, pickling salt, soft water, and seasonings are the basic ingredients for making pickles.

Pickling Ingredients

Perfect pickles start with perfect *produce*. Select young, tender vegetables and firm, ripe fruit. When pickling cucumbers, select a variety specially grown for pickling; the salad variety doesn't make a crisp pickle. If you don't grow your own cucumbers, purchase them from a farm or produce stand where they are harvested daily.

Prepare and process produce as soon after harvesting as possible. Wash fruits and vegetables in cold water. Sort them according to size, shape, and color. Can those of uniform size and shape together to ensure even processing and an attractive, uniform pack. Misfits can be used for relishes.

Vinegar is the key ingredient in pickling. It should be 4 to 6 percent acetic acid, sometimes labeled 40 to 60 grain strength. Most commercial vinegars are a standard 5 percent acetic acid. The acidity is very important because many pickles and relishes are made from low-acid vegetables. Use undiluted vinegar unless a recipe specifies otherwise.

Distilled white vinegar gives pickles a sharp, tart taste, while cider vinegar lends a mellower, fruity flavor. Malt or wine vinegars also may be used, though these vinegars will contribute a distinctive color and flavor to the pickled product. Homemade vinegars vary in acid strength, so reserve them for salads. Buy vinegar by the gallon when you put up a lot of pickles—you'll save money.

Sugar balances the tartness of vinegar. White sugar is most commonly used in recipes, but brown sugar is sometimes called for in relishes and chutneys. If you desire, you can substitute honey for up to half the sugar in a recipe. Pickles also can be made with sugar substitutes; however, there are many differences between products such as Sucaryl and Saccharin, and they should be used according to their manufacturers' directions.

Salt is both a preservative and a flavoring. Pickling salt, which is sold in 5-pound bags at most supermarkets, is preferred. When you can't find pickling salt, pure granulated salt is the next best, and is completely satisfactory. Iodized and plain table salt are undesirable because they contain additives that may cloud brine and discolor pickles.

Water dissolves the salt and provides the liquid in a brine solution. Although soft water doesn't run from the tap in some areas, it's a necessity for pickling. The minerals in hard water may cloud pickling liquid, cause sediment to fall to the bottom of jars, or shrivel pickles. If you live in a hard-water area, try pickling with distilled water. Or boil the hard water for 15 minutes, let it stand for 24 hours, and skim off the surface scum. Then, draw water from the top of the pot so that sediment in the bottom is left undisturbed.

In years past, *powdered alum* and *slaked lime* were added to make pickles crisp and firm. Today, alum and lime are unnecessary when good-quality ingredients are used and up-to-date methods are followed. *Coloring agents*, which alter natural vegetable colors, also are not recommended.

Spices and herbs are the flavor-makers, and here your imagination is the limit. Spices and herbs are always best when they're fresh, but dried and powdered forms are usable. (Use only about one-fourth as much of a dried spice or herb as of fresh, and about one-eighth as much of powdered.) Spices and herbs can be added loose to mixtures that are later strained or can be combined in a bag of muslin or cheesecloth. The spice bag is then used like a tea bag.

Fresh dill is a key ingredient in dill pickles. Other recipes often call for whole peppercorns, cloves, cinnamon stick, ginger, turmeric, mustard seed, and garlic.

Pickling spice, a blend of aromatic spices and peppers, is often called for in recipes. It can be purchased in bottles at the supermarket and can also be made easily at home. To concoct your own, use the following recipe and list of spices as a start. Let your taste buds be your guide.

Pickling Spice

6 cinnamon sticks (3 in. long each), coarsely crushed

3 tablespoons white mustard seed

1 tablespoon *each* whole black peppercorns, cloves, dill seed, whole coriander, and whole allspice

1 tablespoon whole mace, coarsely crushed

A 1-1/2-inch piece ginger root, peeled and finely chopped

1 bay leaf, crumbled

1 dried hot red pepper, crumbled

Combine spices and store in an airtight jar.

Yield: About 2/3 cup.

Spice Possibilities:

Allspice	*Coriander*
Bay leaf	*seed*
Black pepper	*Dill seed*
Cardamom	*Ginger*
Cayenne	*Mace*
Chili	*Mustard*
Cinnamon	*Nutmeg*
stick	*Hot red*
Clove	*pepper*

To make a spice bag, tie together with string a combination of herbs in a square of cheesecloth.

Quick Pickling and Long-Term Brining

Pickling can be a short- or long-term process. Most of today's pickle recipes employ the *fresh-pack,* or *quick-pickling, method* because it's so easy and fast. Cooks who have never attempted pickling are amazed at the speed and simplicity of making delicious pickles this way. In just a few hours you can complete the entire job and enjoy the benefits for weeks and months to come.

Vegetables and fruits, as well as relishes and chutneys, are put up by the fresh-pack method, yet each requires a slightly different preparation and treatment. This chapter features recipes for all these pickles. Some vegetables are marinated in brine from several hours to overnight. The pickles are

then heated, packed into jars, and covered with hot brine. Pickled Cocktail Onions and Pickled Peppers (pages 72 and 73) are examples of this method. Other recipes, such as Dill Spears and Dilly Beans (pages 69 and 73), require no brining at all. Instead, the fresh vegetables are packed directly into the jars, then covered with hot brine. The pickling process takes place in the jar.

Fruits are not usually subjected to a brining process. Instead, they are simmered, and sometimes steeped, in a spicy sweet-and-sour syrup and then transferred with the hot syrup into jars. Relishes and chutneys are prepared in much the same way as fruits.

Brining or *fermentation pickling* is a slower, more time-consuming method.

Sometimes it takes up to 6 weeks. Homemade Sauerkraut and Old-Fashioned Brined Dill Pickles (pages 82 and 83) are made by the long brining fermentation process. Although brining may seem time-consuming at first reading, when you consider that the procedures are spread out over a long period and require only minutes each day, then it seems a less burdensome task and more of a challenge.

Processing Pickles

Generations ago, pickles were packed in jars, but they weren't heat-processed. Many home canners believed that the high concentration of vinegar or salt in pickled foods was enough to prevent spoilage. Today, canning experts agree with the U.S. Department of Agriculture that it is necessary to heat-process most pickled products to arrest enzyme activity and kill bacteria that may cause food spoilage. Heat-processing is not necessary 100 percent of the time, however. Sauerkraut, for example, can be stored for several months without processing when it's kept cool in a large crock in the refrigerator. And foods that are simply marinated in vinegar and seasonings and eaten within a few days need not be heat-processed.

Pickles are processed in a boiling-water bath in much the same way as fruits and tomatoes. Refer to Chapters 2 and 4 (pages 14 and 45) to familiarize yourself with this procedure.

Pickled fruits and vegetables, relishes, and chutneys need to be processed in a boiling-water bath. Processing time varies, depending on the recipe.

Recipes are the heart and soul of pickling. In general modern recipes (such as those in this book) that use up-to-date techniques are more likely to yield quality

A

pickles. Great Aunt Tillie's Bread-and-Butter Pickles may be a family favorite, but the recipe as it has been passed down probably doesn't state a processing time. Also, 25 years ago vinegar contained less acetic acid than it does now, so you may find Aunt Tillie's recipe to be too vinegary. In the following chapter we'll feature many classic family recipes that have been adapted to modern methods. Bread-and-Butter Pickles on page 70 is a delicious example.

Be creative in flavoring pickled products with herbs and spices, but do not alter a recipe's basic ingredients. The correct ratio of vinegar to other ingredients will ensure the safety and quality of the finished product.

The basic steps to fresh-pack pickling are presented below. The steps are only a guide; the recipes that follow will be your blueprint to tasty results.

Detecting Spoilage

Be on the alert for signs of spoilage. Before opening a jar, examine it closely. A bulging lid or leakage may mean that the contents are spoiled. After opening, look for other signs of spoilage, such as spurting liquid, mold, off-odors, discoloration, or an unusual softness or slipperiness to the pickled product. When there is even the slightest sign of spoilage, *do not eat* or even taste the contents. Dispose of the food immediately. After emptying the jar, wash it in hot, soapy water, then boil the jar in water for 15 minutes. See page 11 for a more complete discussion of food spoilage.

B

Step-by-Step Method for Fresh-Pack Pickling

1. *Prepare the jars.* Wash and rinse canning jars, lids, and rings. Keep jars hot—in a low (200°F) oven or in hot water—until they are ready to be used. This will prevent the jars from cracking when they're filled with hot food. Scald metal lids and rings following the manufacturer's directions. Leave lids in the water until they're ready to be used.

2. *Prepare food and pack jars.* Wash produce and prepare as recipe directs. Pack food into hot jars, leaving headspace indicated in recipes. **(Photo A.)**

3. *Seal the jars.* When packing whole vegetables or fruits in brine or syrup, run a narrow spatula gently around the insides of the jars to release any bubbles. Wipe rims clean, place lids on jars with sealing compound next to the glass, and screw on the metal bands firmly, but not too tightly. **(Photos B and C.)**

4. *Process the jars.* Place filled jars on a rack in a water-bath canner or deep, covered kettle filled with hot, but not boiling, water. Arrange jars on the rack so they do not touch each other or the sides of the canner. Add hot water (cold water may crack jars) as needed to cover the jar tops with an inch or two of water. Cover the canner and bring the water to a boil. Start counting the processing time when the water reaches a boil. Process the jars for the time stated in the recipe. At altitudes above 3,000 feet, add 2 minutes' processing time for each additional 1,000 feet.

5. *Cool the jars.* Remove jars with a jar lifter and cool on a cooling rack or folded towel in a draft-free place. Leave space between the jars for air to circulate.

C

6. *Test for a seal.* To test the seal, press down the center of each lid with your finger. Properly sealed lids will stay down. When a jar does not seal by the time it cools completely, refrigerate and eat the contents within a few days.

Like wine, most pickles improve with age—but their flavor doesn't take quite as long as a wine's to mature. Several weeks of "jar aging" will blend the flavors nicely. Label, and store pickles in a cool, dark, dry place. Once opened, refrigerate pickled foods with their liquid covering the contents.

CUCUMBER PICKLES

Many people think only of cucumbers when they consider pickling. After all, they are the classic pickling ingredient. Whether you grow your own or buy them from a produce stand, select varieties known as "picklers" that are grown just for pickling. Their texture, shape, and flavor are superior to other varieties for canning, and they are good for table use, too.

Picklers can be harvested at any size. Harvest small picklers for dill or sweet gherkins. As cucumbers become more mature, they can be crosscut for bread-and-butter pickles or sliced lengthwise for dill spears.

Put up picklers within 24 hours of harvesting. Held longer, they may produce hollow or soft pickles. Wash picklers before you pickle them, but don't scrub so hard that you remove the tiny "prickles." Instead, ensure cleanliness by soaking them in a bath of cold water.

Dill Spears

    4 pounds pickling cucumbers, washed and blossom ends removed
    3 cups white or cider vinegar
    3 cups water
1/3 cup salt
    3 peppercorns per quart
    2 dill heads (or 2 table-spoons dill seed) per quart
    1 garlic clove per quart

1. Cut cucumbers into spears.

2. Combine vinegar, water, and salt in a small saucepan and bring to a boil.

3. Add peppercorns, dill (or dill seed), and garlic to each clean, hot quart jar.

4. Pack cucumber spears in jars.

5. Fill the jars with the boiling pickling mixture, leaving 1/2-inch headspace; seal.

6. Process in boiling-water bath 20 minutes.

Yield: About 3 quarts.

Oil Cucumber Pickles

    2 quarts (about 25) pickling cucumbers, washed and blossom ends removed
1/2 cup salt
1/4 cup whole mustard seed
1/2 teaspoon celery seed
1/8 teaspoon pepper
1/4 cup sugar
1/4 cup olive oil
    3 cups white vinegar

1. Slice cucumbers crosswise into 1/2-inch-thick slices and layer in a bowl with salt. Cover with cold water and allow to stand overnight.

2. Drain cucumbers and rinse with cold water. Drain and rinse again. Set aside to drain completely.

3. Combine remaining ingredients and bring to a boil. Remove from heat.

4. Pack cucumbers into clean, hot jars. Pour hot liquid over them, leaving 1/2-inch headspace; seal.

5. Process in boiling-water bath 10 minutes.

Yield: 4 pints.

In less than an hour you can prepare 3 quarts of fresh-pack Dill Spears.

Quick Dill Pickles

8 pounds small pickling cucumbers, washed and blossom ends removed

3/4 cup salt

1 quart vinegar

1 quart water

2 heads dill (or 1 table-spoon dill seed) per quart

3 peppercorns per quart

1 small, dried hot red pepper per quart (optional)

1 clove garlic per quart (optional)

1. For whole pickles, select cucumbers up to 4 inches long. Larger cucumbers should be halved lengthwise.

2. Combine salt, vinegar, and water; bring to a boil.

3. Pack spices into bottom of clean, hot quart jar. Then pack in cucumbers. Pour boiling brine over pickles, leaving 1/2-inch headspace; seal.

4. Process in boiling-water bath 10 minutes for halved cucumbers; 20 minutes for whole cucumbers.

Yield: 6 quarts.

Bread-and-Butter Pickles

8 cups sliced pickling cucumbers

Salt

2 cups sliced onions

4 green bell peppers (with red on them if possible)

2 cups distilled white vinegar

2 cups sugar

2 teaspoons dry mustard

2 teaspoons turmeric

2 teaspoons celery seed

1 stick cinnamon (broken)

1 tablespoon salt

1. Sprinkle cucumber slices with salt and let soak 1 hour. Wash off with cold water and drain.

2. Cut onion slices cross-wise and the pepper in about 1-1/2-inch lengths (remove seeds).

3. Combine vinegar, salt, sugar, and spices in large kettle and add the cucumbers, onions, and peppers. Bring to a boil and cook 3 to 5 minutes or until cucumbers start to look glassy.

4. Pack pickles into clean, hot jars, leaving 1/2-inch headspace; seal.

5. Process in boiling-water bath 5 minutes.

Yield: 5 to 6 pints.

Fresh-Pack Dill Pickles

Crunch a crisp dill pickle with a noontime sandwich.

3 quarts water

1 quart cider vinegar

1/2 cup salt

1 head fresh dill per quart

1 clove garlic per quart

1/2 teaspoon mixed pickling spice per quart

5 pounds small pickling cucumbers, washed and blossom ends removed

1. Combine water, vinegar, and salt in pot and allow to simmer.

2. Place dill, garlic, and pickling spice in bottom of each clean, hot quart jar. Pack in cucumbers. (It's best to do one jar at a time, from packing to sealing, so that jars and contents remain hot throughout process.)

3. Pour simmering vinegar solution over cucumbers, leaving 1/2-inch headspace; seal.

4. Process in boiling-water bath 20 minutes.

Yield: About 4 quarts.

Sweet Gherkins

A relish tray is not complete without some sweet gherkins.

5 quarts (about 7 lb) 1-1/2- to 3-inch pickling cucumbers, washed and blossom ends removed

1/2 cup salt

8 cups sugar

6 cups distilled white vinegar

3/4 teaspoon turmeric

2 teaspoons celery seed

2 teaspoons whole pickling spice

8 pieces cinnamon stick (1 in. each)

1/2 teaspoon fennel seed (optional)

1 teaspoon vanilla (optional)

1. *First day:* In morning, place cucumbers in a large bowl and cover with boiling water; let stand 6 hours. In afternoon, drain and cover again with fresh boiling water; let stand overnight.

2. *Second day:* In morning, drain cucumbers and cover with fresh boiling water; let stand 6 hours. In afternoon, drain cucumbers; add salt; cover with fresh boiling water.

3. *Third day:* In morning, drain cucumbers; prick with fork. Combine 3 cups of the sugar, 3 cups of the vinegar, and herbs and spices (except vanilla) in a pan. Heat to the boiling point and pour over cucumbers.

In afternoon, drain into a large pan; add 2 cups of the sugar and 2 cups of the vinegar. Heat to the boiling point and pour over pickles.

4. *Fourth day:* In morning, drain into a large pan; add 2 cups of the sugar and 1 cup of the vinegar. Heat to boiling and pour over pickles.

In afternoon, prepare jars. Drain syrup off pickles into large pan; add remaining 1 cup sugar and the vanilla (if desired) to syrup; heat to boiling. Pack pickles into clean, hot jars. Cover with hot syrup, leaving 1/2-inch headspace; seal.

5. Process in boiling-water bath for 10 minutes.

Yield: 7 to 8 pints.

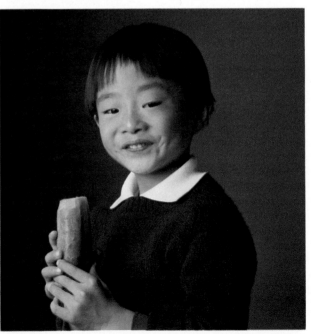

For a nutritious snack, give a child a crunchy pickle.

Pickles and ice cream—perfect for those "expecting."

Crosscut Pickle Slices

This is the perfect pickle for hamburgers and hot dogs.

> 4 quarts (about 6 lb) medium pickling cucumbers, washed, blossom ends removed, and crosscut into 1/4-inch slices

1-1/2 cups small white onions, peeled and sliced

2 large garlic cloves, peeled

1/3 cup salt

2 trays ice cubes

4-1/2 cups sugar

1-1/2 teaspoons turmeric

1-1/2 teaspoons celery seed

2 tablespoons mustard seed

3 cups distilled white vinegar

1. Place cucumbers, onions, and garlic in a large bowl; add salt and mix thoroughly. Cover with ice cubes. Let stand 3 hours. Rinse and drain well; remove garlic; set aside.

2. Combine remaining ingredients in a large pot; heat just to boiling. Add drained cucumber and onion slices to pot and simmer 5 minutes.

3. Pack pickles into clean, hot jars, leaving 1/2-inch headspace; seal.

4. Process in boiling-water bath 10 minutes.

Yield: 7 pints.

Sour Pickles

> 8 pounds (64 to 72) 4- to 6-inch pickling cucumbers, washed and blossom ends removed

3 quarts cider vinegar

3 cups water

3/4 cup salt

3/4 cup sugar

1/2 cup white mustard seed

4 peppercorns per quart

1. Pack cucumbers into clean, hot jars. You may need to cut some cucumbers to pack jars tightly.

2. Combine vinegar, water, salt, sugar, and mustard seed; bring to a boil. Pour boiling liquid over cucumbers, leaving 1/2-inch headspace. Add peppercorns to each jar; seal.

3. Process in boiling-water bath 10 minutes.

Yield: 6 to 7 quarts.

PICKLED VEGETABLES

Following the quick, fresh-pack method, you can pickle every kind of vegetable imaginable—from artichokes to zucchini. Pickled vegetables cut into thin slices add a zesty flavor to salads or sauces; or serve them as an hors d'oeuvre on a relish tray or as an accompaniment to cold meats. They're wholesome and refreshing.

Pickled Beets

> 2 quarts 2-inch-diameter beets (about 15)

1-1/3 cups sugar

2-1/2 cups white or cider vinegar

1 cup water

2 teaspoons whole allspice

1 cinnamon stick, broken

1 teaspoon salt

1. Wash beets, leaving tap roots and 2 to 3 inches of stem attached. Cook in boiling water until just tender (20 to 30 minutes); plunge into cold water; remove skins, stems, and roots.

2. Combine remaining ingredients in a large pot; simmer 15 minutes.

3. Pack beets into clean, hot jars, leaving 1/2-inch headspace. (Cut larger beets in two if necessary.)

4. Return liquid to boil and pour over beets, leaving 1/2-inch headspace; seal.

5. Process in boiling-water bath 30 minutes.

Yield: 4 pints.

Zucchini Pickle

Turn a garden full of zucchini into crisp bread-and-butter pickles. For a change of pace, try this recipe using other summer squash.

> 2 medium onions, thinly sliced

2 red or green bell peppers, skinned and seeded

2 quarts crosscut zucchini (1/2-in.-thick slices)

1/4 cup salt

2-1/2 cups white or cider vinegar

2 cups sugar

1 teaspoon dry mustard

1 teaspoon turmeric

2 teaspoons celery seed

1 cinnamon stick, broken up

1. Cut onion slices in half. Cut peppers into 1/4-inch by 1-1/2-inch strips.

2. Combine zucchini, onions, and peppers and sprinkle with salt; cover with water and let stand 2 hours.

3. Drain vegetables; rinse with cold water; drain thoroughly.

4. Combine vinegar, sugar, and remaining ingredients in a large pot. Bring to a boil; reduce heat and simmer 10 minutes.

5. Add vegetables and return to boil. Remove from heat immediately.

6. Quickly ladle vegetables and liquid into clean, hot jars, leaving 1/2-inch headspace; seal.

7. Process in boiling-water bath 10 minutes.

Yield: 4 pints.

Dilly Beans

Green or wax beans may be used in this recipe. Mix the two for color interest.

4 pounds green beans

6 tablespoons salt

3 cups distilled white vinegar

3 cups water

1/2 teaspoon dill seed (or 1 fresh head dill) per pint

1/2 teaspoon mustard seed per pint

3 whole peppercorns (or 1/4 teaspoon hot red pepper, crushed) per pint (optional)

1 clove garlic, peeled, per pint (optional)

1. Trim beans and remove strings or use whole small beans.

2. Combine salt, vinegar, and water; bring to a boil.

3. Add seasonings to each clean, hot jar. Pack beans in jars; cover with boiling liquid, leaving 1/2-inch headspace; seal. (Beans must be completely covered with liquid.)

4. Process in boiling-water bath 10 minutes.

Yield: 7 pints.

Spiced Beets

Beets lend themselves to pickling in all stages of development. Here we pickle tiny, immature-size beets, leaving them whole.

3 pounds small (approximately 2-in.) beets

1 pound small white onions

1-1/2 cups sugar

1-1/2 cups water

1-1/2 cups cider vinegar

These pickled vegetables were first blanched, then packed separately into jars of hot, spiced brine. Here they make a refreshing hors d'oeuvre tray. See recipes below.

1/2 teaspoon salt (to taste)

2 teaspoons mustard seed

1 teaspoon whole allspice

1/2 teaspoon whole cloves

2 cinnamon sticks, broken

1. Wash beets and cut off roots, leaving 2 to 3 inches of stem attached. Cook in boiling water 10 to 15 minutes until barely tender; plunge into cold water, slip off skins, and remove stems. (Slice larger beets.) Peel and slice onions.

2. Combine remaining ingredients in a large pot and simmer 10 minutes.

3. Add beets and onions; simmer 5 to 10 minutes or until beets are tender.

4. Pack beets and onions into clean, hot jars; cover with hot spiced brine, leaving 1/2-inch headspace; seal.

5. Process in boiling-water bath 20 minutes.

Yield: 4 to 5 pints.

Pickled Cocktail Onions

Onions are an integral part of many pickled products, but this recipe spotlights them.

5 quarts tiny white onions

1-1/4 cups salt

2-1/2 quarts distilled white vinegar

2-1/2 cups sugar

4 tablespoons mustard seed

3 tablespoons whole black peppercorns

4 tablespoons grated horseradish

1 small red pepper per pint

1 bay leaf per pint

1. Cover onions with boiling water. Let stand 2 minutes. Drain and cover with cold water. Peel.

2. Sprinkle onions with salt and cover with water. Let stand overnight.

3. Drain onions. Rinse well with cold water and drain again.

4. Combine vinegar, sugar, mustard seed, peppercorns, and horseradish in large pot. Boil 2 minutes.

5. Add onions and bring to boil again.

6. Pack onions into clean, hot jars. Add pepper and bay leaf to each jar. Fill with boiling syrup, leaving 1/2-inch headspace; seal.

7. Process in boiling-water bath 10 minutes.

Yield: 7 to 8 pints.

Pickled Peppers

P-Pick a p-peck of p-peppers and p-put up P-Pickled P-Peppers.

3 quarts long red, green, or yellow peppers

1 cup salt dissolved in 3 quarts water

2 cloves garlic

1-1/2 tablespoons prepared horseradish

8 cups white vinegar

1-1/2 cups water

3 tablespoons sugar

1. Cut two small slits in each pepper. (Wear rubber gloves to prevent burning hands. Keep hands away from eyes to avoid irritation.)

2. Pour salt water over peppers and let stand 12 to 18 hours in a cool place. Drain, rinse, and drain thoroughly.

3. Combine remaining ingredients; simmer 15 minutes. Remove garlic.

4. Pack peppers into clean, hot jars; pour hot vinegar mixture over peppers, leaving 1/4-inch headspace; seal.

5. Process pints in boiling-water bath 10 minutes.

Yield: 6 pints.

Pickled Hot Peppers

Size is a good indicator of hotness. Usually, the small varieties pack a hotter punch.

2 quarts jalapeño peppers

2 cups white vinegar

2 cups water

1 teaspoon salt (or to taste)

1. Seed and stem peppers; cut or leave whole. (Small peppers may be left whole with stems intact. To prevent bursting, cut two small slits in whole peppers.)

2. Combine vinegar and water; heat to a simmer. Do not boil.

3. Pack peppers tightly into clean, hot jars. Pour hot vinegar solution over peppers, leaving 1/2-inch headspace.

4. Add salt; seal.

5. Process in boiling-water bath 15 minutes.

Yield: 4 pints.

Note: A clove of garlic and 1/2 teaspoon pickling spice may be added to each jar in Step 4, if desired.

Pickled Cauliflower

3 pounds cauliflower (cut into flowerets or 1-inch pieces)

8 onions, sliced

3 tablespoons salt, dissolved in 2 quarts water

1 small, dried hot red pepper

3 whole cloves

1/2 cup sugar

3/4 teaspoons ground turmeric

3/4 teaspoon celery seed

1-1/2 teaspoons white mustard seed

1-1/4 cups white vinegar

1-1/4 cups water

1. Place vegetables in a bowl; cover with salt water; let stand overnight.

2. Next day, drain and rinse vegetables several times with cold water. Set aside.

3. Tie hot pepper and cloves in cheesecloth bag. Add spice bag to remaining ingredients in a large pot; bring to a boil and boil 5 minutes.

4. Add vegetables and cook until barely tender (about 5 minutes). Don't overcook.

5. Remove spice bag. Pack cauliflower and onions into clean, hot jars, leaving 3/4-inch headspace. Cover with boiling liquid, leaving 1/2-inch headspace; seal.

6. Process in boiling-water bath 15 minutes.

Yield: 5 pints.

Italian Pickled Mushrooms in Wine Vinegar

Tantalize the taste buds with these attractive pickled fungi.

3/4 cup lemon juice

6 cups water

8 cups small mushrooms, washed

1/4 teaspoon dried oregano (or 1/2 teaspoon chopped fresh oregano) per half-pint

1/4 teaspoon dried basil (or 1/2 teaspoon chopped fresh basil) per half-pint

1 small bay leaf per half-pint

1 clove garlic per half-pint (optional)

6 cups red or white wine vinegar

1. Combine lemon juice and water in a large pot. Add mushrooms and bring to a boil; reduce heat and simmer 5 minutes. Drain off liquid.

2. Place herbs and mushrooms in clean, hot jars.

3. Bring vinegar to a boil; pour over mushrooms in jars, leaving 1/2-inch headspace; seal.

4. Process in boiling-water bath 20 minutes.

Yield: 8 half-pints.

Note: To vary the flavor, substitute tarragon for the herbs suggested above.

Mustard-Pickled Vegetables

1 quart small cucumbers, cut crosswise in 1/2-inch slices

1 quart small green tomatoes, cut in wedges

2 red bell peppers, cut in 1-1/2-inch pieces

2 green bell peppers, cut in 1-1/2-inch pieces

1 quart small pickling onions, peeled

3 cups (about 1 small head) cauliflower, separated into small flowerets or 1-inch pieces

3/4 cup salt

4 quarts water

1/2 cup flour

1-1/2 cups sugar

1 tablespoon turmeric

1/2 cup cold water

1/2 cup Dijon-style mustard

5 cups vinegar

1. Place cut-up vegetables in a large bowl. Dissolve the salt in the 4 quarts water and pour over vegetables. Allow to stand 8 to 10 hours in a cool place.

2. Drain off brine. Rinse vegetables and drain thoroughly.

3. Place flour, sugar, and turmeric in a large pot; gradually stir in cold water until smooth. Add mustard and vinegar, and cook until the sauce thickens and coats a spoon.

4. Add drained vegetables and simmer 15 minutes.

5. Pack into clean, hot jars, leaving 1/4-inch headspace; seal.

6. Process in boiling-water bath 10 minutes.

Yield: About 8 pints.

PICKLED FRUITS

The imaginative pickler can capture an orchard in a jar—everything from the familiar peaches and pears to exotic mangoes and papayas.

Spicy Oranges

Hot or cold roasted meats and spicy oranges are a dynamic duo.

    7 oranges
    2 cups sugar
3/4 cup malt vinegar
2/3 cup water
    1 cardamom pod, outer pod removed (optional)
   10 cloves
1/4 teaspoon black peppercorns
    2 cinnamon sticks, broken in half
1/2 teaspoon whole allspice
1/8 teaspoon salt

1. Place whole oranges in a pot; cover with warm water. Bring to a boil, reduce heat, and simmer until the peel is tender (30 to 45 minutes).

2. Remove from heat; drain oranges and allow to cool.

3. In a saucepan, combine sugar, vinegar, and 2/3 cup water. Tie spices in a spice bag and add to saucepan. Bring to a boil; reduce heat and simmer for 10 minutes. Remove syrup from heat, discard spice bag, and set aside.

4. Slice oranges; remove seeds. If oranges are large, cut slices in half. Add orange slices to syrup and bring to a boil over medium heat. Lower heat and simmer for 20 minutes.

5. With slotted spoon, lift oranges from syrup and carefully pack into clean, hot jars. Pour hot syrup over oranges, leaving 1/2-inch headspace; seal. (If desired, add a piece of cinnamon stick and a few cloves to each jar before sealing.)

6. Process in boiling-water bath 10 minutes.

Yield: About 6 pints.

Note: Allow to mature 3 weeks before using.

Spiced Mangoes

Gently spiced, this tropical fruit has a deliciously mysterious flavor.

1-1/2 quarts peeled, sliced mangoes
    3 tablespoons whole cloves
    1 tablespoon whole allspice
    3 tablespoons mace blades (or 1/4 teaspoon ground mace)
1-1/2 cups white wine vinegar
1-1/2 cups water
    6 cups sugar
    3 peppercorns per pint

1. Peel, seed, and slice the mangoes to measure 1-1/2 quarts.

2. Tie spices (except peppercorns) in a cheesecloth bag. Combine vinegar, water, sugar, and spice bag in a large pot. Bring to a boil; reduce heat and simmer 5 minutes.

3. Add mangoes and simmer until slightly translucent (about 5 minutes).

4. Remove spice bag. Pack mangoes in clean, hot jars. Add peppercorns to each jar and cover mangoes with hot syrup, leaving 1/2-inch headspace; seal.

5. Process in boiling-water bath 20 minutes.

Yield: About 4 pints.

Spiced Plums

    6 pounds plums
    7 cups sugar
    2 cups water
    2 cups red wine vinegar
    4 cinnamon sticks
1/4 cup whole cloves

1. Wash plums and prick each one with a needle or toothpick in several places to prevent bursting.

2. Place sugar and water in a large pot; bring to a boil and simmer 10 minutes. Add vinegar, cinnamon, and cloves; boil 5 minutes.

3. Add plums and slowly bring to a boil. Skim off foam that rises to the surface. Remove pot from heat and allow plums to stand in syrup 12 to 24 hours in a cool place.

4. Bring plums and syrup to a boil; reduce heat and simmer 3 to 5 minutes.

5. Pack hot plums into clean, hot quart jars. Pour hot syrup over plums, leaving 1/2-inch headspace; seal.

6. Process in boiling-water bath 10 minutes.

Yield: About 4 quarts.

Note: Allow plums to mature for 4 to 6 weeks before serving.

Spiced Plums with a dollop of cream make a tempting and easy dessert.

Crabapple Pickles

2 quarts (about 2-1/2 lb) crabapples

1-1/2 tablespoons whole cloves

1-1/2 tablespoons whole allspice

2 cinnamon sticks, broken

6 cups sugar

3 cups vinegar

3 cups water

1. Wash crabapples. Do not peel. Run a large needle through each to prevent bursting.

2. Tie spices in a cheesecloth bag. Combine remaining ingredients in a large pot and add spice bag. Bring to a boil; boil 5 minutes.

3. Add apples. Bring to a simmer and cook apples until tender. Remove from heat and allow to stand 12 to 18 hours in a cool place.

4. Remove spice bag. Pack apples in clean, hot jars. Heat syrup to boiling and pour over apples, leaving 1/2-inch headspace; seal.

5. Process pints or quarts in boiling-water bath 15 minutes.

Yield: 6 pints or 3 quarts.

Gingered Peach Pickles

These peaches are delicious over ice cream or served with crème fraîche.

8 pounds (about 3-1/2 qt) small peaches

3 pounds light brown sugar

1 quart cider vinegar

A 1-inch piece ginger root, peeled and crushed

2 tablespoons whole cloves, crushed

3 cinnamon sticks, broken up

1 whole clove per peach

1 cinnamon stick per quart

1 tablespoon brandy per quart (optional)

1. Peel peaches and treat to prevent darkening. (See page 43.) Halve and pit or leave whole.

2. Combine sugar and vinegar in a large pot; bring to a boil over medium heat and boil 5 minutes. Tie ginger root, crushed cloves, and broken cinnamon sticks loosely in cheesecloth. (See page 67.) Add to syrup and simmer 5 minutes.

3. Stick a whole clove in each peach. Add only enough peaches to the boiling syrup to fill one of the quart jars; cook until peaches are hot but not soft (about 2 minutes). Do not overcook. Remove peaches with slotted

Gingered Peach Pickles are rich and spicy, with a slight hint of brandy.

spoon and pack tightly in clean, hot jar with a small stick of cinnamon. Repeat process until all peaches are packed in jars.

4. Bring syrup to a boil; remove spice bag. Pour hot syrup over peaches in jars, leaving 1/2-inch headspace. Add 1 tablespoon brandy to top of each quart jar, if desired. Seal.

5. Process in boiling-water bath 15 minutes.

Yield: 3 to 4 quarts.

Pickled Figs

These figs make a surprisingly delightful accompaniment to steaks or chops.

3 quarts whole figs

2 quarts boiling water

1 cup water

6 cups sugar

1 cup vinegar

2-1/2 teaspoons *each* whole pickling spice, whole cloves, and cinnamon sticks (broken)

1. Place figs in pan or bowl and cover with boiling water; let stand 5 minutes.

2. Combine 1 cup water, sugar, and vinegar in a large pot; bring to a boil. Tie spices in a cheesecloth bag and add to syrup.

3. Drain figs well; add to spiced syrup and simmer for 10 minutes. Let stand overnight in syrup in a cool place.

4. Repeat simmering in syrup once a day for next two days. Remove spice bag.

5. Immediately bring figs and syrup to a boil. Pack figs into clean, hot jars and cover with syrup, leaving 1/2-inch headspace; seal.

6. Process in boiling-water bath 10 minutes.

Yield: 6 pints.

Watermelon Pickles

Here's the ultimate example of letting nothing go to waste. These pickles are crisp, with a delightful sweet-tart flavor.

3 quarts watermelon rind, cut in 1-inch squares

3/4 cup salt

3 quarts water

2 trays ice cubes

1 tablespoon whole cloves

3 cinnamon sticks, broken in half

8 cups sugar

3 cups white vinegar

3 cups water

1 lemon, thinly sliced and seeds removed

1. Remove the outer green and inner pink portions from rind. Cover pared rind with brine made from salt and 3 quarts water. Add ice and let stand 6 hours.

2. Drain; rinse with cold water; drain again. Place rind in pot, cover with cold water, and cook until just tender (about 10 minutes). Do not overcook. Drain.

3. Tie spices in a cheesecloth bag. Combine sugar, vinegar, 3 cups water, and spices; boil 5 minutes. Remove spice bag, retaining cinnamon sticks. Pour syrup over watermelon rind and add lemon slices. Let stand overnight.

4. Heat watermelon rind and lemon slices in syrup to boiling; cook until rind is translucent (about 10 minutes).

5. Pack hot rind into clean, hot jars. Add 1 piece cinnamon stick from the spice bag to each jar. Cover with boiling syrup, leaving 1/2-inch headspace; seal.

6. Process in boiling-water bath 10 minutes.

Yield: 4 to 5 pints.

RELISHES

There are no limits to the combinations of vegetables, fruits, and seasonings that can be turned into tantalizing relishes. By varying the amounts of mustard and spices to vinegar, you can make a relish as mild or hot as you like. Decreasing the cooking time will make a more crisp relish. The next few pages of recipes should get you started.

Chow Chow

This zesty relish is an all-American favorite; it adds great flavor to hamburgers, as well as to many other dishes, and it's simple and fun to make.

    1 small head cabbage, cored
    1 medium head cauliflower
    2 medium onions, peeled
    2 green bell peppers, seeded
1-1/2 pounds green tomatoes
    2 red bell peppers, seeded
    3 tablespoons salt
2-1/2 cups cider vinegar
1-1/2 cups sugar
1-1/2 tablespoons dry mustard
    2 teaspoons turmeric
    1 tablespoon celery seed
    1 tablespoon mustard seed

1. Finely chop vegetables using the coarse blade of a food (meat) grinder or in a food processor. Combine chopped vegetables with salt in a large bowl. Let stand about 6 hours in a cool place. Drain well.

2. Combine remaining ingredients in large pot and simmer 10 minutes.

3. Add drained vegetables; simmer 10 minutes. Bring to a boil.

4. Quickly pack into clean, hot jars, leaving 1/2-inch headspace; seal.

5. Process in boiling-water bath 10 minutes.

Yield: About 5 pints.

Green Tomato Mincemeat

This is a marvelous sweet condiment dubbed "mincemeat." It takes 3 hours of simmering, but it is not hard to make and is well worth the time spent. Use it like traditional mincemeat—in pies, cookies, and served warm over vanilla ice cream. A shot of brandy or rum added to the warmed mincemeat lends a festive touch.

    6 cups peeled, chopped apples
    6 cups chopped green tomatoes
    4 cups light brown sugar
1-1/4 cups cider vinegar
    2 cups golden raisins
    3 teaspoons ground cinnamon
    1 teaspoon ground cloves
 3/4 teaspoon ground allspice
 3/4 teaspoon ground mace
    2 teaspoons salt
 1/2 teaspoon freshly ground black pepper
 1/2 cup butter

1. Mix apples and tomatoes together in large pot. Add remaining ingredients (except the butter).

2. Bring gradually to a boil and simmer for 3 hours, stirring often.

3. Add the butter and mix well. Spoon into clean, hot jars, leaving 1/2-inch headspace; seal.

4. Process in boiling-water bath 25 minutes.

Yield: 5 pints.

Sweet Pickle Relish

    4 cups ground, unpeeled cucumbers (about 4)
    1 cup ground green bell pepper (about 2)
 1/2 cup ground red bell pepper (about 1)
    3 cups finely diced celery
 1/4 cup salt
3-1/2 cups sugar
    2 cups white vinegar
    1 tablespoon celery seed
    1 tablespoon mustard seed

1. Grind vegetables in a food (meat) grinder using the coarsest blade.

2. Combine all vegetables in a large bowl; sprinkle with salt and cover with cold water. Let stand 4 hours. Drain thoroughly in a colander, then press out all liquid.

3. Combine sugar, vinegar, celery seed, and mustard seed. Bring to a boil, stirring until sugar is dissolved. Stir in drained vegetables. Simmer for 10 minutes.

4. Immediately pack into clean, hot jars, leaving 1/2-inch headspace; seal.

5. Process in boiling-water bath 10 minutes.

Yield: About 6 pints.

Dixie Relish

This condiment is an American classic you'll "relish."

    1 head (about 3 lb) cabbage, cored
    6 medium-size white onions, peeled
    6 large red bell peppers, seeded
    6 large green bell peppers, seeded
 1/2 cup salt
    1 tablespoon whole cloves
    1 tablespoon whole allspice
    1 stick cinnamon
    4 tablespoons mustard seed
    3 tablespoons celery seed
    1 quart distilled white vinegar
    3 cups sugar
    1 tablespoon salt

1. Grind vegetables in a food (meat) grinder with coarsest blade or finely chop in food processor. Mix with 1/2 cup salt. Stir well and let stand 3 to 4 hours.

2. Drain in a colander lined with cheesecloth, pressing to remove excess liquid.

3. Tie cloves, allspice, and cinnamon in a cheesecloth bag.

4. Combine vegetables, spice bag, and remaining ingredients in a large pot and simmer 5 minutes. Remove spice bag.

5. Ladle into clean, hot jars, leaving 1/2-inch headspace; seal.

6. Process in boiling-water bath 10 minutes.

Yield: 7 pints.

Piccalilli

This is a great hamburger and hot dog relish.

- 1 quart finely chopped cabbage
- 1 quart finely chopped green tomatoes
- 1 cup finely chopped celery
- 2 large onions, finely chopped
- 2 red bell peppers, seeded and finely chopped
- 2 green bell peppers, seeded and finely chopped
- 1/4 cup salt
- 1 cinnamon stick
- 1 teaspoon *each* whole cloves and whole allspice
- 1-1/4 cups cider vinegar
- 1-1/2 cups water
- 2 cups firmly packed brown sugar
- 1 teaspoon dry mustard
- 1 teaspoon turmeric
- Dash hot pepper sauce

1. Chop vegetables using the coarse blade of a food (meat) grinder or in a food processor. Combine vegetables and salt; cover and let stand overnight.

2. Drain off as much liquid as possible, pressing through a clean, thin white cloth if necessary.

3. Tie cinnamon, cloves, and allspice in a cheesecloth bag.

4. Place vegetables, spice bag, and remaining ingredients in a large pot. Bring to a boil; reduce heat and simmer 20 minutes.

5. Ladle into clean, hot jars, leaving 1/2-inch headspace; seal.

6. Process in boiling-water bath 15 minutes.

Yield: 4 pints.

The recipe for this all-American Sweet Pickle Relish can be found on the opposite page.

Red Pepper Relish

- 16 red bell peppers (about 10 cups ground)
- 4 medium onions, peeled and quartered
- 2 cups white or cider vinegar
- 2 cups sugar
- 1 tablespoon salt
- 1 tablespoon white mustard seed

1. Remove seeds, stems, and cores from peppers. Put peppers and onions through food (meat) grinder using coarsest blade, or chop finely in a food processor.

2. Combine vegetables with remaining ingredients in a large pot. Bring to a boil; simmer 20 minutes, stirring occasionally.

3. Skim foam off surface. Pack into clean, hot jars, leaving 1/2-inch headspace; seal.

4. Process in boiling-water bath 10 minutes.

Yield: About 7 pints.

Zucchini Relish

- 4 cups finely chopped zucchini
- 3 cups finely chopped carrots
- 4 cups finely chopped onion
- 2 cups finely chopped green bell pepper (2 large)
- 2 tablespoons salt (or to taste)
- 2-1/4 cups vinegar
- 3/4 cup dark brown sugar
- 1 tablespoon celery seed
- 1 teaspoon dry mustard

1. Chop vegetables using the coarse blade of a food (meat) grinder or in a food processor. Combine all ingredients in a large pot. Cook 10 minutes or until vegetables are just tender but still crisp.

2. Immediately pack into clean, hot jars, leaving 1/2-inch headspace; seal.

3. Process in boiling-water bath 20 minutes.

Yield: 6 to 7 pints.

Green Tomato Relish

This relish is crisp, tart, and complements all sorts of dishes.

- 2 cups coarsely ground green tomatoes (4 or 5 medium)
- 2 cups peeled and coarsely ground cucumbers (2 medium)
- 2 cups peeled and coarsely ground onions (4 medium)
- 3 medium-size tart apples, peeled and coarsely ground
- 1 green bell pepper, seeded and coarsely ground
- 2 small red bell peppers, seeded and coarsely ground
- 4 cups water
- 1-1/2 tablespoons salt
- 2 cups white sugar
- 2 cups cider vinegar
- 1 tablespoon mustard seed
- 6 tablespoons all-purpose flour, sifted
- 1 tablespoon dry mustard, sifted
- 1/4 teaspoon turmeric

1. Grind green tomatoes, cucumbers, onions, apples, and green and red peppers in a food (meat) grinder, using the coarsest blade.

2. Place vegetable mixture in a large pot; add water and salt. Let stand for 24 hours.

3. Drain liquid off vegetables. Add sugar, 1-1/2 cups of the vinegar, and mustard seed. Bring to a slow boil and cook 30 minutes, stirring occasionally.

4. Sift flour, mustard, and turmeric together. Stir in remaining 1/2 cup vinegar to make a smooth paste. Stir paste into boiling vegetable mixture.

5. Simmer for an additional 30 minutes or until mixture has thickened, stirring occasionally.

6. Fill clean, hot jars, leaving 1/2-inch headspace; seal.

7. Process in boiling-water bath 10 minutes.

Yield: About 4 pints.

Corn Relish

Straight from the field, fresh corn can be transformed into a superb relish.

- 22 medium-size ears of corn (enough to make 10 cups kernels)
- 1 cup chopped red bell peppers (1 large pepper)
- 1 cup chopped green bell peppers (1 large pepper)
- 1-1/4 cups chopped celery
- 3/4 cup chopped onions
- 1-1/2 cups sugar
- 2-1/2 cups distilled white vinegar
- 2 cups water
- 1 tablespoon salt
- 1 teaspoon celery seed
- 2-1/2 tablespoons mustard seed
- 1/2 teaspoon ground turmeric

1. Cook ears of corn in boiling salted water for 3 to 5 minutes. Plunge into cold water.

2. Drain corn. Cut kernels from cob with knife. Kernels should measure 10 cups.

3. Combine corn with remaining ingredients in large pot and simmer 15 minutes.

4. Immediately pack into clean, hot pint jars, leaving 1/2-inch headspace; seal.

5. Process in boiling-water bath 15 minutes.

Yield: 5 to 6 pints.

CHUTNEYS

Mention chutney and mouths water for spicy East Indian dishes. However, chutney, a spicy combination of fruits with herbs and spices, is equally delicious with barbecued meats, roasts, fowl, chops, or cold cuts. In India, chutney is served fresh, but here it's more often preserved.

Sweet-Hot Mixed-Fruit Chutney

This chutney is delicious with cream cheese and toasted almonds on crackers for a fast hors d'oeuvre.

- 1 teaspoon *each* whole peppercorns, whole allspice, mustard seed, whole cloves, and celery seed
- 2-1/4 cups sugar
- 1 cup distilled white vinegar
- 1 cup water
- 2 fresh green hot chiles, seeded and chopped (or 1 dried hot red chile)
- 1/2 teaspoon ground ginger
- 3 medium apples, peeled, cored, and finely chopped
- 2 peaches, nectarines, or mangoes, peeled, seeded, and finely chopped
- 1 lemon, peeled and finely chopped
- 1 orange, peeled and finely chopped
- 1 onion, peeled and finely chopped
- 1/3 cup sliced blanched almonds

1. Tie the peppercorns, allspice, mustard seed, cloves, and celery seed in cheesecloth bag. Combine sugar, vinegar, water, spice bag, and chiles in a large pot.

2. Add fruits and onion and simmer 20 minutes. Add almonds; cook 10 minutes more or until desired thickness is reached. Remove spice bag.

3. Pack into clean, hot jars, leaving 1/2-inch headspace; seal.

4. Process in boiling-water bath 20 minutes.

Yield: 4 half-pints.

Red bell peppers add a sweet flavor to pickled foods.

Red and Green Tomato Chutney

This is a hot chutney, perfect with Indian curry dishes.

1/3 cup peeled, grated ginger root

1/3 cup chopped garlic

1-1/2 tablespoons salt

3 pounds firm tomatoes, chopped (some green, some red, or all green)

3-1/2 cups brown sugar

2-1/4 cups distilled white vinegar or red wine vinegar

2 teaspoons cayenne

3 teaspoons Garam Masala (recipe follows)

1. Grind ginger root, garlic, and salt with a mortar and pestle.

2. Combine ground spices, tomatoes, and remaining ingredients in a large pot; cook over medium heat about 1 hour, stirring occasionally.

3. Pack into clean, hot jars, leaving 1/2-inch headspace; seal.

4. Process in boiling-water bath 10 minutes.

Yield: 5 half-pints.

Garam Masala: Grind together finely with mortar and pestle black seeds from 1 cardamom pod (discard pod), 1/2 teaspoon whole cloves, 15 black pepper-corns, 1 teaspoon cumin seed, and a 1-inch piece of cinnamon stick.

Chutney, a complex blend of fruit and spices in a pungent sauce, is a classic accompaniment to Indian curry dishes. With time, the flavors in chutneys blend and soften. For a tasty snack, try chutney on crackers with cream cheese.

Mango Chutney

Major Grey move over!

1 cup distilled white vinegar

3-1/4 cups sugar

6 cups peeled, sliced green mangoes (about 10 medium)

1/4 cup peeled, freshly grated ginger root

1-1/2 cups raisins

2 chile peppers, seeded and finely chopped

1 clove garlic, minced

1/3 cup sliced onion

1/2 teaspoon salt

1. Boil vinegar and sugar in a large pot for 5 minutes.

2. Add remaining ingredients and cook about 30 minutes or until thick.

3. Pack into clean, hot jars, leaving 1/2-inch headspace; seal.

4. Process in boiling-water bath 10 minutes.

Yield: 8 half-pints.

Cranberry-Orange Chutney

6 medium oranges

1 pound cranberries

2 cups sugar

1/4 cup finely chopped crystallized ginger

1/8 teaspoon cayenne

1 stick cinnamon (2 in.)

1 clove garlic, peeled

1/2 teaspoon curry powder

3/4 cup raisins

1. Remove outer peel (colored part only) from 4 oranges. Slice peel into thin strips to make 1/4 cup. Cut off white membrane and slice oranges 1/4-inch thick. Remove seeds and quarter slices. Reserve pulp. Juice remaining 2 oranges to make 1/2 cup juice.

2. Combine orange peel, juice, and remaining ingredients (except orange pulp) in a 4-quart or larger pot. Cook over medium heat, stirring until sugar dissolves and cranberries burst. Remove pot from heat.

3. Remove cinnamon stick and garlic. Stir in reserved orange pulp.

4. Ladle into clean, hot jars, leaving 1/4-inch headspace; seal.

5. Process in a boiling-water bath 10 minutes.

Yield: 6 half-pints.

Helen's Peach Chutney

Peaches make a lighter, less rich chutney than the one using mangoes. This condiment is excellent with delicately flavored meats such as veal and chicken.

1/2 cup chopped green bell peppers

1/2 cup chopped white onions

3 or 4 small hot chiles, seeded and finely chopped

1/2 unpeeled lime or lemon, very finely chopped

1 clove garlic, minced

2 cups white sugar

1 cup brown sugar

1 cup distilled white vinegar

1 cup golden raisins or currants

1/2 teaspoon dry mustard

1/2 teaspoon salt

1 teaspoon ground allspice

1-1/2 teaspoons ground ginger

4 pounds peaches, peeled, pitted, and chopped

1. Combine all ingredients except peaches in a large pot; bring to a boil.

2. Add peaches; simmer 45 minutes.

3. Pack into clean, hot jars, leaving 1/2-inch headspace; seal.

4. Process in boiling-water bath 10 minutes.

Yield: 5 to 6 pints.

Lemon Chutney

This recipe, which is delicious with curries, calls for fenugreek, an unusual Indian spice that can be found at ethnic and specialty food stores.

Juice and slivered peel of 8 lemons

3 onions, chopped

1-1/4 cups golden raisins

1 green bell pepper, finely chopped

1 dried hot red pepper

4 large peaches, peeled, pitted, and chopped

2 cups sugar

1 teaspoon ground coriander

1/2 teaspoon ground fenugreek (optional)

1/2 teaspoon ground cloves

1 teaspoon salt

1. Combine all ingredients in a large pot and simmer slowly for about 45 minutes. Mash slightly before canning.

2. Pack into clean, hot jars, leaving 1/2-inch headspace; seal.

3. Process in boiling-water bath 10 minutes.

Yield: 6 half-pints.

Mango-Peach-Cantaloupe Chutney

2 cups white vinegar

5 cups light brown sugar

2 teaspoons whole cloves

1 teaspoon ground allspice

1-1/2 teaspoons ground nutmeg

7 cups chopped onions (about 2-1/2 lb)

1 cup raisins

1 cup black currants

2 tablespoons peeled, minced fresh ginger root

1-1/2 tablespoons minced garlic

6 cups peeled, sliced peaches (about 3 lb)

4 cups peeled, sliced mangoes (about 2-1/2 lb)

4 cups peeled, sliced firm cantaloupe (about 2-1/2 lb)

1. Combine vinegar, sugar, and spices in a large pot. Bring to a boil; reduce heat and simmer 45 minutes.

2. Add onion, raisins, currants, ginger, and garlic. Cook over medium heat for 15 minutes.

3. While syrup is cooking, prepare and measure fruits.

4. Add fruits to pot. Bring to a boil; reduce heat and simmer for about 2 hours, stirring occasionally. Chutney may be cooked until desired thickness is reached.

5. Ladle into clean, hot jars, leaving 1/2-inch headspace; seal.

6. Process in boiling-water bath 10 minutes.

Yield: 7 pints.

Black Chutney

1 pound (about 20) Damson plums

2 cups brown sugar or dark corn syrup

1/2 cup cider vinegar

1-1/4 cups raisins

10 pitted prunes, cooked

1 apple, peeled, cored, and diced

1/16 teaspoon cayenne

1/2 teaspoon *each* ground allspice, cloves, pepper, cardamom, and ginger

1. Cover plums with water in a large pot and cook until soft. Remove pits.

2. Combine pitted plums with remaining ingredients in a large pot. Cook slowly about 30 minutes or until desired consistency is reached.

3. Pack into clean, hot jars, leaving 1/2-inch headspace; seal.

4. Process in boiling-water bath 20 minutes.

Yield: 3 to 4 half-pints.

Apricot and Curry Chutney

1-1/2 pounds dried apricots, chopped (4 cups chopped)

1 quart water

1-1/2 cups chopped onion

1/2 cup sugar

3 cups golden raisins

3 cups white vinegar

1-1/2 tablespoons grated fresh ginger

1-1/2 to 2 teaspoons curry powder

2 cinnamon sticks (2 in. *each*)

3/4 teaspoon salt

1. Combine apricots, water, onion, and sugar in a 6-quart

pot and simmer 5 minutes, stirring occasionally. Add remaining ingredients the last 10 minutes of cooking.

2. Remove cinnamon sticks and ladle into clean, hot jars leaving 1/2-inch headspace; seal.

3. Process in a boiling-water bath 10 minutes.

Yield: About 4 pints.

Apple-Raisin Chutney

3 quarts peeled, cored, and chopped tart apples (about 8 lb)

1 cup chopped onions

1 cup chopped red bell peppers (1 large)

2 cloves garlic, minced

3 cups raisins

4 cups firmly packed brown sugar

1 quart cider vinegar

2 dried hot red peppers (or 1-1/2 tablespoons dried red pepper flakes)

3 tablespoons yellow mustard seed

2 teaspoons ground ginger

2 teaspoons ground allspice

2 teaspoons salt

1. Combine all ingredients in a large pot; bring to a boil. Reduce heat and simmer 1 hour and 15 minutes, or until thick. As mixture thickens, stir frequently.

2. Ladle into clean, hot jars, leaving 1/2-inch headspace; seal.

3. Process in boiling-water bath 10 minutes.

Yield: 7 to 8 pints.

Celebrate the German Octoberfest with a Sauerkraut-making party. Assign individual tasks to friends. Keep guests happy by serving good German beer.

Fermentation Pickling

Brined pickles, including sauerkraut, undergo a curing process of about 3 to 6 weeks. During fermentation, the bacterial yeast naturally present in food feeds on natural sugar, converting it to lactic acid. Lactic acid gives sauerkraut, for example, that snappy, sharp taste that vinegar can almost, but not quite, duplicate.

Fermentation pickling requires careful attention. The process takes place most effectively at a temperature of around 70°F. Lower temperatures will slow the process; higher temperatures will cause premature fermentation and possible spoilage.

Salt preserves the pickles as they ferment. The proper amount of salt in the brine solution is a key factor in making good pickles. Too much salt may arrest fermentation and too little will cause the pickles to soften and have an unappetizing flavor. All fermented pickles must be completely submerged in brine. Air is a villain that causes spoilage, so be sure that at least 2 inches of brine covers the food. Use an earthenware crock with a crack-free glaze. New brine of the original strength can be added when necessary.

From top left: 1) Cut heads into quarters, then shred cabbage. 2) Sprinkle it with salt. 3) Press cabbage into crock. Brine will form. 4) Cover cabbage with plastic bag filled with water.

Homemade Sauerkraut

Sauerkraut can be served cold in salads or hot with meats. From start to finish you can make your own kraut in 3 to 6 weeks.

Late-harvest cabbage is the best for sauerkraut because it's highest in natural sugar.

To make a smaller quantity of sauerkraut, reduce the recipe ingredients proportionately and proceed as directed. Allow 2 ounces salt to each 6 pounds of cabbage.

50 pounds cabbage

1 pound salt

1. Let cabbage heads stand at room temperature for about 24 hours to wilt. This causes the leaves to soften slightly and become less likely to break when cut Wash the heads and remove outer leaves. Cut heads into quarters and remove the cores.

2. With a sharp knife, shred 5 pounds of cabbage 1/8- to 1/4-inch thick.

3. Place the shredded cabbage in a large mixing bowl and sprinkle with about 3 tablespoons of the salt. Mix the salted cabbage with your hands or with a stainless steel spoon and let it stand 3 to 5 minutes.

4. Wash a 10-gallon crock with soapy water, rinse, and scald it with boiling water. Pack the salted cabbage into the crock. A brine will form as you press the cabbage down. Repeat the shredding and salting in 5-pound lots until the crock is filled to within no more than 5 inches of the top. The brine should cover the cabbage. If it does not, add additional brine by heating 1-1/2 tablespoons of salt with 1 quart of water. Cool the brine to room temperature before adding it to the crock.

5. To cover the cabbage and weight it down to keep it submerged in the brine: Fill a clean, large, heavy plastic bag, such as a heavy-duty trash bag, with water and lay it over the cabbage. Fit the bag snugly against the inside walls of the crock to prevent the surface of the cabbage from being exposed to air. (This will prevent the growth of a yeast film or mold.) Add more water to the plastic bag, if necessary, to keep the cabbage submerged. Seal the bag.

6. Cover the crock with plastic wrap, or its lid.

Fermentation will take from 3 to 6 weeks depending on the room temperature. The ideal temperature is 75°F. At 75°F fermentation will take about 3 weeks; at 70°F, 4 weeks; at 65°F, 5 weeks; and at 60°F allow about 6 weeks.

Keep track of the temperature so you know when to check the sauerkraut. After the allotted time, remove the cover. Fermentation is complete if no bubbles rise when the crock is tapped gently.

7. Tightly packed in covered containers, the kraut can be safely kept in the refrigerator for several months. However, if you don't have refrigerator space, consider canning the sauerkraut.

To can, bring the kraut to a simmer; do not boil. Pack it into clean, hot jars, leaving 1/2-inch headspace; seal. Process in a water-bath canner 20 minutes for quarts or 15 minutes for pints. Start counting the processing time when the water in canner starts to boil.

Yield: 16 to 18 quarts.

Old-Time Sauerkraut Method:
Many long-time kraut makers still make sauerkraut the old-fashioned way. The advantage is that you can check and taste the kraut as it ferments, and stop the fermentation process when it suits your taste. The disadvantage is that the sauerkraut requires daily attention.

After packing the crock with salted cabbage, place a piece of thin, white cloth (such as muslin) directly over the cabbage and tuck the edges down against the inside of the container. Cover the cabbage with a heavy plate that fits snugly inside the container so that the cabbage is not exposed to air. Put a weight on top of the plate so that the cabbage is fully immersed in the brine. A glass jar filled with water makes a good weight. The brine should come up 2 inches above the plate—this makes daily skimming easier. Make additional brine if necessary, as directed above.

Cover the crock with a clean terry-cloth towel and top with plastic wrap to prevent evaporation. Tie string around the crock to hold the towel and plastic wrap in place. Remove the scum daily from the surface with a scalded stainless steel spoon. Replace the cloth and plate with a clean one. Cover the crock again with the towel and plastic wrap.

This method takes about the same length of time as the previous one.

The sauerkraut is done when bubbles stop rising to the surface. Taste the kraut. When it suits your taste, remove it from the crock. Refrigerate the kraut in covered containers or pack it into jars and process as described above. Makes 16 to 18 quarts.

Pickling Problem Solver

Problem	Cause	Prevention
Soft or slippery pickles (spoilage—do not eat)	1. Brine or vinegar was too weak.	1. Use pickling salt, and vinegar of 4 to 6 percent acidity. Follow recipes that employ up-to-date techniques.
	2. Pickles were not completely covered with brine.	2. Pickles should be covered with liquid at all times, during the brining process and when in jars.
	3. Scum was not removed from top of brine during long-term brining.	3. Scum should be removed daily during the brining process.
	4. Pickles were not processed long enough to destroy spoilage organisms.	4. Follow the recommended method of processing for the recommended length of time.
	5. Seals were not airtight.	5. Check jars for nicks and cracks before using. Always use new metal lids.
	6. Cucumbers were pickled with blossom ends attached.	6. Remove blossom ends when washing cucumbers.
	7. Fermentation or storage area too warm.	7. Ferment pickles at temperatures no higher than 75°F. Store pickled foods in a cool (under 70°F), dry place.
Shriveled, tough pickles	1. Too much salt, sugar, or vinegar was added to cucumbers at one time.	1. Start with a weaker solution of brine, sugar, or vinegar and gradually add the full amount called for in the recipe.
	2. Hard water.	2. Use soft water.
	3. Produce not fresh.	3. Pickle produce within 24 hours of havesting.
White sediment falls to bottom of jars of firm pickles (Pickles are still edible.)	1. Harmless yeast has grown on the surface and settled.	1. None.
	2. Hard water.	2. Use soft water.
Dark, discolored pickles (Pickles are still edible.)	1. Hard water.	1. Use soft water.
	2. Iron, brass, or copper cookware used.	2. Prepare and cook pickled foods in enamel-ware, glass, earthenware, or stainless steel.
	3. Table salt used (contains additives).	3. Use pickling salt.
Hollow cucumbers	1. Not pickled when fresh.	1. Pickle cucumbers as soon as possible after harvesting.
	2. Too rapid fermentation of pickles.	2. Fermentation should occur ideally at 75°F, or at lower temperatures.

These dill pickles are cured for three weeks in a crock before they're canned.

Old-Fashioned Brined Dill Pickles

For a strong garlic flavor, add 10 to 20 garlic cloves to the pickling brine. For a mild garlic flavor, add a garlic clove to each jar of pickles before processing.

    20 pounds pickling
        cucumbers, 3 to 6
        inches long
    3/4 cup whole mixed
        pickling spice
    2 to 3 bunches fresh dill
    2-1/2 cups vinegar
    1-3/4 cups salt
    2-1/2 gallons water

1. Cover cucumbers with cold water and wash thoroughly but gently. Remove blossom ends. Drain and wipe dry.

2. Place half the pickling spice and a layer of dill in a 5-gallon crock or glass container.

3. Fill the crock with cucumbers to within no more than 5 inches of the top. Place a layer of dill and the remaining pickling spice over the top of the cucumbers.

4. Mix the vinegar, salt, and water and pour it over the cucumbers.

5. Cover the cucumbers with a heavy plate that fits inside the crock. Place a weight on the plate to keep the cucumbers submerged and completely covered with brine. Cover the crock loosely with a clean cloth.

6. Keep the pickles at room temperature, ideally at 75°F. In about 3 to 5 days scum will start to form on the brine. Remove it daily with a metal spoon.

7. Do not stir pickles. Always keep them completely submerged in brine. Add more brine as necessary, following the original proportions of vinegar to salt to water.

8. After 3 weeks of fermentation, the dills will be ready to be put up in jars. At this point, the brine may be cloudy due to the development of yeast during the fermentation period. Strain the brine, or make a fresh brine of 1/2 cup salt and 4 cups vinegar to 1 gallon water. (The strained brine makes a better pickle because its flavors have blended with the cucumbers and dill.) Bring the brine to a boil.

9. Pack the pickles, along with some of the dill from the crock, into clean, hot quart jars. Do not pack too tightly.

10. Cover the pickles with hot brine, leaving 1/2-inch headspace; seal.

11. Process in boiling-water bath 15 minutes.

Yield: 9 to 10 quarts.

Specialties of the House

A distinctive collection of gourmet preserved delicacies you're sure to enjoy preparing as well as eating. Share them with your friends—they make perfect gifts everyone will appreciate receiving.

This chapter is a hodge-podge of recipes that are fun and a bit out of the ordinary. Many of these epicurean delicacies line the shelves of specialty food shops. But why pay gourmet prices when you can make them for about half the cost and have fun at the same time?

For family and friends who love good food, nothing will please them more than a jar of homemade Berry Syrup or Coarse-Ground mustard (pages 88 and 92).Packed in a decorative container and tied with a big, bright bow, either makes a delightful gift from your kitchen.

Many of the following recipes borrow ideas and rely on techniques presented in earlier chapters of this book. So before you get started, it will help if you skim through the previous chapters, particularly Chapters 2. Many of the recipes call for sterilizing jars. To refresh your memory about sterilization methods, see pages 16 and 17.

Use your imagination to decorate containers of food gifts. Use pine cones, ribbons, spices, wooden utensils, baskets, pretty labels, and fancy jars.

HERBS AND FLAVORED VINEGARS

There's nothing like the heady aroma and pungent flavor of fresh herbs. Grow some indoors or out, or seek sources of fresh ones grown in your area. In addition to using herbs as flavor accents, preserve their freshness by this simple pickling process. You'll be able to enjoy the flavor of fresh herbs the year around.

To use herbs preserved in vinegar, remove desired amount, rinse in cold water, chop, and add to recipe.

Herb Vinegar

Enhance plain vinegars with the flavor of your favorite herb or spice. The following method can be used with any herb or spice. Use about 4 ounces of fresh herbs or 2 ounces of dried herbs per quart of vinegar.

Tarragon sprigs (or other fresh herb)

White wine or rice vinegar

1. Wash fresh tarragon and pat dry with paper towels. Place a few sprigs in each sterilized bottle.

2. Pour vinegar into bottles and cap tightly.

3. Allow herbs to steep in vinegar for 5 to 6 weeks before using.

Herbs in Vinegar

The French tightly pack tarragon leaves in little jars, then completely fill the jars with vinegar.

This method works with any leafy herb. Some herbs that are nice to have on hand are basil, thyme, tarragon, oregano, dill weed, and rosemary.

Enough sprigs of a fresh herb to fill jar

White wine vinegar (to cover)

1. Wash herbs and dry with paper towels or in salad spinner.

2. Pack herbs into hot, sterilized jars.

3. Heat vinegar just to the boil. Pour over herbs, leaving 1/8-inch headspace. Cap tightly.

Note: Refrigerate jars after opening.

For gourmet flavor, enhance commercial vinegars with fresh garden herbs.

Fran's Raspberry Vinegar

Use this raspberry vinegar in salad dressings, when poaching pears or apples, or to deglaze the sauté pan in which chicken or veal has been browned. This vinegar mellows as it ages. It keeps indefinitely—improving with time. Store the vinegar in a cool, dark, dry place and refrigerate after opening.

12 baskets raspberries (6 oz *each*)

  cup sugar

 2 quarts or more good-quality red or white wine vinegar

1. Rinse berries and place in large sterilized glass jars.

2. In a saucepan, combine sugar and vinegar and bring to a boil, stirring until sugar dissolves.

3. Pour hot vinegar over berries. Berries must be completely covered with vinegar; if not, add more to cover. Cover loosely and let stand in a cool place 3 to 4 weeks.

4. Strain mixture through a fine sieve into a saucepan, pressing gently to extract juice from berries. Bring liquid to a boil, reduce heat, and simmer 10 minutes, skimming off foam.

5. In the meantime, boil canning jars or glass bottles, completely immersed in water, 15 minutes to sterilize. (Any type of bottle that will withstand the boiling temperature needed to sterilize it may be used.)

6. Ladle hot vinegar into hot bottles, leaving 1/4-inch headspace; cap tightly.

Yield: 2 quarts.

Ceviche is made from raw fish marinated in lime juice. The juice "cooks" the fish, so that it looks and tastes as though it has been poached.

PICKLED FISH

Pickled Herring

 2 pounds salt herring fillets

3/4 cup water

3/4 cup white vinegar

 1 bay leaf

1/4 teaspoon black peppercorns

1/4 teaspoon whole allspice

1/4 teaspoon dill seeds (or 1 sprig fresh dillweed)

1/2 cinnamon stick

1/3 cup sugar

 1 red onion

1. Soak the fillets in a bowl of cold water in the refrigerator for 12 to 24 hours. Change water twice.

2. To make the pickling solution, combine water, vinegar, seasonings, and sugar in a saucepan; bring to a boil. Stir to dissolve sugar. Let cool.

3. Rinse the fillets with cold water and pat dry with paper towels. Cut fish in 1-inch pieces.

4. Peel and slice onion. Separate slices into rings.

5. Arrange herring and onion rings in alternate layers in sterilized jars. Cover with pickling solution and cap.

6. Refrigerate 3 to 6 days before serving. The herring will keep up to 3 weeks refrigerated.

Yield: 2 pints.

Pickled Herring in Cream

This is best when prepared the day before it is to be served. Make only as needed because the sauce loses its thick, creamy texture when it stands several days.

 1 pint Pickled Herring (preceding recipe)

1/4 cup sour cream

1/4 cup heavy cream

1. Drain the pickled herring and onion. Reserve the pickling liquid.

2. Combine the sour cream and cream. Stir in a fourth of the reserved pickling liquid.

3. Add the herring and onions, and return to the jar. Cover and refrigerate overnight.

Yield: 2 cups.

Ceviche

This makes a delightful appetizer or luncheon entrée. Serve it with lettuce, hard egg slices, tomato wedges, and avocado.

 1 pound firm, white fish (rock cod, red snapper, turbot, or mackerel)

 Juice of 3 limes

 1 tomato, peeled, seeded, and diced

 1 avocado, peeled, pitted, and diced

 3 green onions, thinly sliced

 2 small garlic cloves, minced

 2 fresh or canned Serrano or jalapeño chiles, seeded and finely chopped

 2 tablespoons oil

 Fresh chopped cilantro (to taste) or 1/2 teaspoon dried oregano

 Cilantro or parsley sprigs, for garnish

 Lime wedges, for garnish

1. Remove bones from fish, if necessary, and cut into small cubes.

2. Place fish in a glass or ceramic bowl and cover with lime juice. Cover the bowl with plastic wrap and allow fish to marinate 4 hours or overnight in the refrigerator, stirring it several times.

3. Drain fish and mix with remaining ingredients.

4. Serve cold. Garnish each serving with a sprig of cilantro or parsley and a wedge of lime.

Yield: 4 to 6 servings.

Marinated Prawns

These prawns make terrific hors d'oeuvre and are attractive served on ice for a cocktail party.

3 pounds prawns, peeled and deveined

1 lemon slice per pint

1 bay leaf per pint

Poaching liquid:

1 quart water

1/4 cup salt

1/2 cup white vinegar

2 bay leaves

1/2 teaspoon *each* mustard seed, whole allspice, and whole cloves

1 teaspoon dried red hot pepper flakes

1 teaspoon white peppercorns

Pickling brine:

3 cups water

1-1/2 cups white wine vinegar

1 tablespoon sugar

2 teaspoons mixed pickling spice

1. Bring the poaching liquid to a boil; simmer 20 minutes.

2. Wash prawns and add to poaching liquid; simmer 5 minutes. Remove prawns to cool. (This liquid may be discarded or used to poach other fresh fish.)

3. Simmer pickling brine for 10 minutes. Cool.

4. Pack prawns in sterilized jars. Add bay leaf and lemon slice to each pint jar. Cover with pickling brine to top of jar; seal.

5. Refrigerate 1 week before serving.

Yield: 2 pints.

An office lunch of corned beef on rye with mustard and pickle is hard to beat. See the Quick Corned Beef recipe below.

PICKLED MEATS

Pickling is probably the safest method of preserving meats at home. But unless you eat pickled meat within a few days, it must be canned. Refer to the information on canning meats in Chapter 5, which begins on page 55.

Pickled Pigs' Feet

Some people love them, so here's a way to put them up at home.

Pigs' feet

Salt

Vinegar solution:

2 quarts vinegar

1/2 teaspoon hot red pepper flakes

2 tablespoons grated horseradish

1 teaspoon whole black peppercorns

1 teaspoon whole allspice

1 bay leaf

1. Scald, scrape, and clean the feet thoroughly. Sprinkle lightly with salt and let stand 4 to 8 hours.

2. Wash feet well with water. Place them in a large pot, cover with hot water, and cook until meat is tender but not until meat can be removed from bones.

3. Prepare vinegar solution in a pot; bring to a boil.

4. Pack feet in clean, hot jars, leaving 1-inch headspace. Cover with boiling vinegar solution, leaving 1/2-inch headspace; seal.

5. Process pints or quarts in pressure canner 75 minutes at 10 pounds pressure for altitudes up to 2,000 feet. (See chart, page 55, for higher altitudes.)

Virginia's Quick Corned Beef

Here's a quick method for producing a flavorful corned beef without the preservatives added to the commercial product. It's ready to cook and serve within 3 days.

4 quarts cold water

1-1/2 cups coarse (kosher) salt

1 tablespoon light brown sugar

2 tablespoons pickling spice

6 whole peppercorns

3 bay leaves

1 tablespoon cream of tartar (optional)

6 pounds fresh boned beef (brisket, rump, bottom round, or eye of round)

1. Combine all ingredients except meat in large pot. (Cream of tartar may be added to the brine to preserve the meat's pinkish color. It's a good substitute for the preservative saltpeter. Without a preservative ingredient, the meat will have a grayish color.) Bring to a boil, reduce heat, and simmer 10 minutes. Cool to room temperature.

2. Place beef in scalded glass, ceramic, or enameled crock. Pour cooled brine over meat. Weight down the meat with a heavy plate and a heavy weight (such as a glass jar filled with water). Meat must be completely submerged in liquid.

3. Cover container and store in a cool place for 2 to 14 days. A temperature of less than 40°F is advisable.

4. To cook corned beef: Wash off meat. Simmer for 3 or more hours in seasoned water or stock until tender. Serve warm or cold.

Concoct luscious sundaes and splits with homemade berry syrups.

FRUITS AND NUTS

Tutti-Frutti

Tutti-frutti is best started in the late spring, at the beginning of the fresh-fruit season.

1 quart California brandy (at least)

  Strawberries, hulled, washed, and drained

  Bing cherries, pitted

  Peaches, peeled and pitted

  Plums, halved and pitted

  Apricots, halved and pitted

  Pears, peeled and cored

  Pineapple, pared and cut in chunks

  Sugar

1. Begin by pouring the brandy into a large crock or jar (at least a gallon). Add fruits in season and *their weight in sugar* (one pound fruit to one pound sugar). After each addition of fruit and sugar, cover the crock and let it stand in a cool place. Fruits should always be covered by brandy, so add more if necessary.
2. As fruits come into season, add them to the crock with an equal weight of sugar.
3. When the crock is full, cover tightly and let it stand in a cool place for 3 months before using.

Berry Syrup

Strawberries, blueberries, blackberries, and many other berries make delightful syrups. They are delicious on pancakes or waffles or as dessert sauces.

4 pounds berries

2 cups water

  Sugar

  Lemon juice

1. Wash berries and place in a large pot. Add water and crush berries to start juices flowing. Bring to a simmer and simmer 2 to 3 minutes. Do not boil.

2. Pour juice and pulp through a jelly bag or cheesecloth-lined colander suspended over a bowl. Let juice drain and squeeze bag to extract all possible juice.

3. Measure juice and return it to pot. To each cup juice, add 2/3 cup sugar and 1 teaspoon lemon juice.

4. Bring syrup to a simmer and simmer 5 to 10 minutes.

5. Ladle into clean, hot jars, leaving 1/4-inch headspace; seal.

6. Process in boiling-water bath 10 minutes.

Yield: About 6 pints.

Note: If you end up with jelly instead of syrup, it's because the berries used were high in pectin. Simply reheat the jellied syrup and thin with water. If the syrup is not thick enough, boil it in a saucepan to reduce and thicken it.

Chestnuts in Rum Syrup

Chestnuts in syrup make a delicious topping for vanilla ice cream (*Coupe aux Marrons*). They are also used in many French or Italian pastries.

2-1/2 cups fresh chestnuts, shelled and peeled

3-3/4 cups water

  1/2 cup light brown sugar

  3/4 cup granulated sugar

  1/2 cup corn syrup

  1 vanilla bean, split lengthwise

  2 to 4 tablespoons dark rum or cognac

1. To shell chestnuts: With a sharp knife, cut slits or crisscross gashes in the flat sides of the chestnuts and drop into boiling water for 2 to 3 minutes. While the chestnuts are still warm, remove the shells and inner skins, using a sharp knife. If any chestnuts are still difficult to peel, return them to the boiling water for a minute longer.

2. Cover peeled chestnuts with water and simmer until just tender. Allow to cool in cooking liquid.

3. Drain nuts. Leave whole or cut in quarters.

4. Combine water, sugars, corn syrup, and vanilla bean in a saucepan. Bring to a boil and boil 2 to 3 minutes.

5. Add chestnuts to syrup and simmer until nuts are very tender and syrup is reduced by one-half, about 20 to 25 minutes. Remove from heat.

6. Remove vanilla bean. Add liquor. Pack chestnuts and syrup into hot, sterilized containers, leaving 1-inch headspace. Cap tightly.

7. Chestnuts in rum syrup may be stored in the refrigerator for up to 3 months.

Yield: About 2-1/2 cups.

Grape Leaves, Greek Olives, feta cheese, cracker bread, and white wine make a delightfully different feast.

VEGETABLE SPECIALTIES

Grape Leaves

Approximately 120 whole grape leaves
Water
1/4 cup coarse salt
1 quart water

1. Pick grape leaves when young, tender, and light green. Cut off stems and wash in cold water.

2. Bring water to a boil in a 6-quart or larger pot. Drop in 10 to 12 grape leaves at a time for 30 seconds. Lift grape leaves out and plunge into cold water. Pat leaves dry with paper towels.

3. Stack leaves in piles of 6 and roll up loosely from the long side. Tie each roll with string. Continue this process until all leaves are cooked and rolled up.

4. Pack rolls of leaves in clean, hot pint or quart jars. (About 6 rolls will fit into a quart jar.)

5. Bring salt and 1 quart water to a boil; boil 5 minutes.

6. Pack rolls of leaves vertically into 3 quart jars, bending them gently to fit below the shoulders of the jars.

7. Cover with hot brine, leaving 1/8-inch headspace; seal.

8. Process in boiling-water bath 15 minutes.

Yield: 3 quarts.

To use: Untie the rolls and rinse in cold water. Use in any recipe calling for grape leaves. Refrigerate after opening.

Roman-Style Artichokes in Oil

These flavorful, rich artichokes make a hearty vegetable addition to meals. Prepare when the artichoke supply reaches its peak between March and May. Look for artichokes with compact, green heads and tightly closed leaves.

75 very small (under 3 in. in diameter) artichokes
1-1/2 cups lemon juice
3 quarts water
Vinegar
Water
1 clove garlic per pint
1/2 teaspoon dried basil (or 1 teaspoon chopped fresh basil) per pint
1/4 teaspoon dried mint (or 1/2 teaspoon chopped fresh mint) per pint
6 cups olive oil

1. Remove outer leaves from artichokes; cut off bud tops and stem ends (leave 1-1/2-inch stem if possible). Wash thoroughly.

2. In a large pot, combine lemon juice and 3 quarts water. Add artichokes, bring to a boil, and simmer 10 minutes. Drain and place artichokes in large bowl or crock. Add equal parts of vinegar and water to cover artichokes. Cover and let stand 10 hours or overnight. Drain brine.

3. Add garlic, basil, and mint to clean, hot jars. Pack in artichokes and cover with oil, leaving 1/2-inch headspace; seal.

4. Process in boiling-water bath 30 minutes.

Yield: 6 pints.

Note: Artichoke hearts may be substituted if small artichokes are unavailable.

Marinated Artichoke Hearts

Keep a jar of artichoke hearts handy in your refrigerator. They add zest to plain salads and taste terrific as a cold hors d'oeuvre.

  2 packages (10-oz each) frozen artichoke hearts
1/2 cup white wine vinegar
1/2 cup water
  4 garlic cloves, peeled
  1 tablespoon salt
1/4 teaspoon dried, crushed thyme
3/4 teaspoon *each* dried basil and oregano
1/8 teaspoon cayenne
    Light, fruity olive oil

1. Steam or boil artichoke hearts. Drain well and pat dry with a paper towel.

2. Place artichoke hearts into four scalded, half-pint jars.

3. Combine remaining ingredients, except olive oil, in a saucepan. Bring to a boil.

4. Pour hot liquid over artichoke hearts. Distribute garlic cloves between jars. Add enough olive oil to each jar to come up to the jar rim.

5. Cap jars and refrigerate artichokes about 1 week before serving. (Artichokes will keep about 2 weeks longer.)

Yield: 4 half-pints.

Jardiniere

Arrange colorful combinations of summer vegetables in clear glass jars. Choose and layer the vegetables to create the most pleasing combinations of colors and shapes. You can simply pack the vegetables in jars raw and cover with brine. However, for uniform crunchiness, certain vegetables should remain raw, some should be

blanched, and others should be parboiled before they are packed and brine is added. See recommendations for specific vegetables in parentheses:

Beans, green or waxed (parboiled)
Bell pepper segments (raw)
Broccoli flowerets (parboiled)
Cabbage pieces (blanched)
Carrot slices or thin strips (parboiled)
Cauliflower flowerets (parboiled)
Celery pieces (raw)
Cucumber slices (raw)
Eggplant pieces (parboiled)
Green cherry tomatoes (raw)
Green tomato slices (raw)
Jerusalem artichoke pieces (raw)
Mushrooms (parboiled)
Okra (blanched)
Onion pieces (blanched)
Radishes (raw)
Whole baby white onions (blanched)
Zucchini slices (raw)

  Vegetables
    1 teaspoon salt per quart
    2 cloves garlic per quart
    3 peppercorns per quart
  1/2 Hot pepper per quart (optional)

  Covering liquid:
    1 part vinegar
    1 part water

1. Select any combination of the above vegetables. Wash and cut in appropriate sizes. Leave vegetables raw or cook as suggested in parentheses.

2. Pack vegetables in colorful layers in clean, hot jars. Add salt, garlic, and peppercorns (and hot peppers if desired) to each jar.

3. Mix water and vinegar. Pour over vegetables, leaving 1/2-inch headspace; seal.

4. Process quarts in boiling-water bath 20 minutes.

TOMATO TANTALIZERS

To the tomato gardener, there's no such thing as too many tomatoes—especially when there's a good cook in the kitchen. Green or red-ripe tomatoes can be transformed into a host of delectable preserves and condiments. Recipes for everything from Red Tomato Jam to Green Tomato Relish are sprinkled throughout the chapters of this book. On page 45 directions are given for canning vine-ripened tomatoes and making tomato sauce and paste.

The following recipes are variations on a theme. Start with a piquant chili sauce and work your way through to tangy catsup.

Chili Sauce

  8 pounds ripe tomatoes
  3 red bell peppers, chopped
  3 green bell peppers, chopped
  1 stalk celery, chopped
  2 cups chopped onions
  2 cloves garlic, crushed
  1 teaspoon *each* whole allspice, mustard seed, and whole cloves
  1 cup light brown sugar
  2 tablespoons salt
  1 teaspoon *each* fresh ground black pepper and dry mustard
  2 dried hot red peppers, crushed
1-1/2 cups cider vinegar

1. Peel, core, and chop tomatoes. Combine tomatoes, red and green bell peppers, celery, onions, and garlic in a large pot. Bring to a boil and simmer 45 minutes.

2. Tie whole spices in a cheesecloth bag and add to tomato mixture. Add sugar, salt, black pepper, mustard, and hot peppers. Boil, uncovered, until thick.

3. Add vinegar and boil the sauce until it has thickened to the desired consistency. Discard spice bag.

4. Pour into clean, hot jars,

leaving 1/2-inch headspace; seal.

5. Process in boiling-water bath for 15 minutes.

Yield: 8 pints.

Tomato Catsup

This homemade tomato catsup is thick and spicy and far superior to store-bought catsup.

 10 pounds ripe tomatoes, peeled and chopped
  3 onions, finely chopped
  2 red or green bell peppers, seeded and chopped
  2 garlic cloves, minced
  1 stick cinnamon (2 in.)
  8 whole black peppercorns
  5 whole cloves
  5 whole allspice
  1 teaspoon whole celery seed
3/4 cup packed dark brown sugar
  1 cup white vinegar
  1 tablespoon salt
  1 tablespoon paprika
1/4 teaspoon or more cayenne

1. Cook tomatoes, onion, peppers, and garlic in a 6-quart or larger pot 30 to 40 minutes, until vegetables are soft.

Spicy Barbecue Sauce (recipe below) makes the best grilled chicken.

2. Purée vegetables in a food processor or press through a food mill.

3. Return purée to the pot and simmer 30 to 40 minutes, until the mixture is reduced by about half.

4. Tie the seasonings together in a cheesecloth bag and add to the tomato mixture.

5. Simmer, stirring frequently to prevent sticking and scorching, until the catsup is very thick. Remove spice bag.

6. Spoon into clean, hot jars, leaving 1/4-inch headspace; seal.

7. Process in a boiling-water bath 10 minutes.

Yield: About 7 pints.

Spicy Barbecue Sauce

A delicious sauce with a Far Eastern touch for barbecued country-style spare ribs or chicken cooked over coals or in the oven.

3/4 pound butter, clarified
  6 cups chopped onion
  6 garlic cloves, chopped
  5 cups fresh or canned tomato purée

  3 cups packed light brown sugar
  1 cup rice vinegar
  1 cup soy sauce
  6 ounces (6 tablespoons) chili paste with garlic (available at Oriental markets)

1. To clarify butter: Melt butter and skim off foam with a spoon. Pour clarified butter into a 6-quart or larger pot. (Discard any white milk solids that have settled in the bottom of the butter pan.)

2. Add onions and garlic to butter and cook 15 minutes, or until onions are golden.

3. Add remaining ingredients. Bring to a boil, reduce heat, and simmer 30 minutes, stirring occasionally.

4. Purée mixture in food processor or press through food mill.

5. Return sauce to pot and simmer 10 to 20 minutes, stirring frequently.

6. Ladle sauce into clean, hot jars, leaving 1/4-inch headspace; seal.

7. Process in a boiling-water bath 20 minutes.

Yield: 5 pints.

SAUCES

Chinese Plum Sauce

  3 red bell peppers
  2 pounds ripe peaches *or* apricots, sliced
  2 pounds plums, sliced
  4 cups cider vinegar
  2 cups water
  1 cup granulated sugar
1-3/4 cups packed light brown sugar
  1/3 cup light corn syrup
  5 large cloves garlic, minced
  6 tablespoons peeled, chopped ginger root
1-1/2 tablespoons coarse (kosher) salt
  3 tablespoons white mustard seed, lightly toasted
  1 small onion, chopped
  2 dried hot red peppers, seeded and crushed
  1 stick cinnamon

1. Place bell peppers under broiler and roast until skin is blistered and lightly charred on all sides. Remove from heat and wrap in a damp towel for 15 minutes. Scrape off skin. Remove seeds and stems. Set aside.

2. Simmer sliced peaches and plums, 2 cups of the vinegar, and the water in a large pot until the fruit is tender (about 20 to 30 minutes). Remove from heat.

3. Combine the remaining 2 cups vinegar, the sugars, and corn syrup in another large pot; stir and bring to a boil.

4. Add the fruit mixture, bell peppers, and remaining ingredients. Cover and simmer 8 minutes. Remove lid and simmer for about 1 hour, stirring occasionally.

5. Remove cinnamon stick and purée mixture through medium disc of food mill to remove skins and fibers. Return sauce to pot and bring to a boil. Continue to boil gently until sauce thickens (10 to 15 minutes), stirring frequently.

6. Ladle hot sauce into clean, hot, half-pint jars, leaving 1/2-inch headspace; seal.

7. Process in boiling-water bath 10 minutes.

Yield: 6 half-pints.

Note: Allow to stand in jars for 1 month before using.

Cajun Hot Sauce

72 small, fresh hot red peppers, stemmed and seeded
  2 cloves garlic, minced
  2 cups water
  2 tablespoons sugar
  1 teaspoon salt
  4 teaspoons grated, fresh horseradish
  2 cups vinegar

1. Combine peppers, garlic, and water in a pot. Cover and simmer until peppers are very tender. Purée in food processor or food mill.

2. Combine puréed peppers with remaining ingredients in a pot. Simmer, stirring occasionally, until mixture thickens.

3. Pour into clean, hot half-pint jars, leaving 1/2-inch headspace; seal.

4. Process in boiling-water bath 10 minutes.

Yield: 3 to 4 half-pints.

Clockwise from bottom left: Coarse-Ground Mustard, Green Peppercorn Mustard, and Homemade Mustard.

MUSTARDS AND HORSERADISH

Coarse-Ground Mustard

1/2 cup white mustard seed

1/2 cup red wine

2/3 cup red wine vinegar

1/2 cup water

1/2 teaspoon ground allspice

1 teaspoon honey

1-1/2 teaspoons minced garlic

3 teaspoons coarse (kosher) salt

2 bay leaves, finely crushed

1. Combine mustard seed, wine, and vinegar in a glass bowl; let stand 4 hours.

2. Place this mixture in a food processor or blender and add remaining ingredients. Process briefly to retain coarse texture.

3. Place in upper part of double boiler and stir over simmering water 10 minutes or until mustard begins to thicken.

4. Place in hot, sterilized jars. Allow to cool; then cap and refrigerate.

Yield: 2 to 3 half-pints.

Homemade Mustard

1/4 cup dry mustard

1/4 cup white wine vinegar

1/3 cup dry white wine

1 tablespoon sugar

1/2 teaspoon salt

3 egg yolks

1. Mix together all ingredients except egg yolks and allow to stand 2 hours.

2. Whisk yolks into mixture. Transfer mixture to the top of a double boiler.

3. Cook, stirring constantly, over hot, not boiling, water, until mustard thickens (about 5 minutes).

4. Cool mustard. Cover and refrigerate up to 1 month.

Yield: 1 cup.

Tarragon Mustard: Add 1/2 teaspoon crushed dried tarragon when adding egg yolks.

Lemon or Lime Mustard: Add 3/4 teaspoon grated lemon or lime peel, and 1-1/2 teaspoon lemon or lime juice when adding egg yolks.

Green Peppercorn Mustard

1/3 cup white mustard seed

2/3 cup dry mustard

1 cup hot water

1 cup white wine vinegar

1 cup dry white wine

1 tablespoon coarse (kosher) salt

1 teaspoon dried tarragon, crumbled

1 teaspoon dill seed

1/8 teaspoon *each* ground cloves and cinnamon (or to taste)

2 teaspoons honey

2 tablespoons green peppercorns, drained (or to taste)

Crushed green peppercorns (optional)

1. Combine mustard seed, dry mustard, water, and white wine vinegar; allow to stand 3 hours.

2. Combine the wine, salt, herbs, and ground spices in a saucepan; bring to a boil. Allow to stand 5 minutes. Strain through fine sieve into the mustard mixture and stir. (Discard spices in strainer.) Stir in the honey and drained green peppercorns.

3. Place in a food processor or blender and purée.

4. Place mustard mixture in top of a double boiler and cook about 10 minutes, stirring frequently.

5. Remove from heat and add a few crushed green peppercorns, if desired.

6. Put into hot, sterilized jars. Allow to cool; then cap tightly. Refrigerate.

Yield: 2 half-pints.

Prepared Horseradish

Horseradish is a novelty in your garden and it's easy to grow. Used judiciously, it is the spirited component of many sauces and condiments and lends a flavorful sharpness to boiled meats, especially corned beef. (See recipe, page 87.)

Prepare horseradish as you need it. Wash and scrub the roots with a stiff brush, peel the outer covering, and trim off any rough spots. When you get to the white meat, grind or grate it in a well-ventilated room—it's potent stuff! Tightly wrap the remainder of the unpeeled root in plastic wrap, and store in the refrigerator. For longer storage, freeze pieces of the whole root or small packets of grated horseradish.

    1 cup grated fresh
      horseradish root
  1/2 cup white, rice, or wine
      vinegar
  1/4 teaspoon salt (to taste)
      Sugar (to taste)
      (optional)

1. Before grating, wash horseradish roots and remove outer brown peel. Grate finely by hand or cut into small cubes and grate in a food processor.

2. Place grated horseradish in a bowl and add vinegar and salt. Add a little sugar to taste, if desired.

3. Pack into small, sterilized jars and cap tightly.

4. Store in the refrigerator.

Note: Horseradish will keep for weeks, but is best when freshly prepared.

HOME-CURED OLIVES

If you've ever tasted an olive right off the tree, you'll know that this fruit is not to be consumed raw like most other fruits. Cured by a lye-and-brine process, olives mellow and develop a subtle and characteristically salty taste. Cured in layers of salt by the Greek-style method, olives wrinkle and take on a strong, slightly bitter flavor, for which you may have to acquire a taste. Once you have, you'll love them!

The procedure for curing olives is simple and straight-forward. Follow the directions carefully and precisely, and don't skip any steps or try to hurry the process. Never can home-cured olives; improperly handled, they can be a dangerous source of food poisoning.

Picking the Fruit

In California and across the Southwest, where olive trees flourish, harvest olives when they mature—usually in late October or early November. If your yard doesn't have a tree, perhaps a neighbor's property or nearby school does. Most people willingly share their olives, because when trees aren't picked, the fruit falls to the ground, creating a messy nuisance.

For green-ripe olives, pick fruit that is pale green, straw yellow, or cherry red. Black fruit is overly mature and will soften too much if cured. To make Greek-style olives, harvest olives that are dark red to black. Small olives are best; the big ones become too soft when cured by this process. To avoid bruising the fruit as you gather it from the tree, place the olives in a basket, old pillowcase, or pail of water. If you can't cure the olives immediately after harvesting, place the fruit in a brine of 3/4 cup salt to 1 gallon of water. They will keep up to 4 days in this brine.

Greek-Style Olives

You'd never know by looking just how delicious Greek-style olives are. On the out-side, their black, shriveled skin looks downright ugly. But their wrinkled exterior hides a juicy, succulent inter-ior. Tossed with tangy feta cheese in salads, or savored out-of-hand, these olives make a tasty treat.

Curing by the Greek process requires a wooden crate or box 18 by 30 inches for each 5 gallons of olives. A lug box such as peaches or other tree fruits are some-times packed in works well. Ask the produce buyer at your local market if he'll give you one in exchange for some homemade olives. You'll need a piece of burlap to line the box, and another piece to cover it. You'll also need a large container to sur-round and hold the wooden box, and a small plastic stor-age container.

Besides olives, table salt and a little olive oil are the only ingredients required. You'll need lots of salt—about 10 pounds (12 cups) for the first layering process, 20 pounds for the second process, and 5 pounds to pack the olives for storage. Fortunately, it's cheap.

Now you're ready to start. Place the wooden box in a larger container. (The first step requires that the brine drain; you'll have a mess if you don't catch the flow.) Line the wooden box with burlap. Lightly sprinkle the olives with water and place them in a single layer over the cloth. Completely cover the fruit with salt and build layers of olives and salt, end-ing with a layer of salt. Place another piece of burlap over the top and tuck in the edges to cover the fruit completely.

Allow the olives to stand for a week in a cool, enclosed area, such as a basement or garage. After a week, remove the cloth and transfer the salty olives to a large container. Pour off the brine and reline the wooden box with burlap. Then layer the olives into the box with more salt, making sure that you add enough salt to coat the fruit thoroughly. It will take several more cups, but don't worry about exact amounts; you can't add too much. Then cover the olives with burlap and let them stand 3 to 4 days.

Repeat this layering process every 3 to 4 days for a month, adding 1 to 2 cups of salt each time. During the process, if mold appears on the stem end, pick out the moldy olives and immerse them in a bowl of vinegar for an hour or so, then return them to the salted olives.

When the olives are shriv-eled and no longer ooze brine, remove them from the box. Bring 2 quarts of water to a boil in a large pot and fill a wire strainer with 1 or 2 cups of fruit. Dip the strainer into the boiling water for about 4 seconds to rinse and seal the olives. Repeat this process, changing the water after every tenth dip or so, until all the olives have been rinsed. Spread them in a single layer on several thick-nesses of paper towels to allow them to dry.

To store, combine each gallon of olives with 1 pound of salt. Layer the salted olives between paper towels (to absorb excess moisture) in a broad, flat-bottomed plastic storage container. Cover and refrigerate Greek-style olives up to 6 months.

Rinse the olives before eat-ing them. Then coat lightly with olive oil and enjoy.

Olives are soaked with lye, thoroughly rinsed, and cut to check color change from lye penetration.

Green-Ripe Olives

Serve homemade olives as you would the store-bought variety. They add color and a succulent flavor to everything from elegant appetizers to everyday casseroles.

To produce green-ripe olives, follow this three-step process developed by the University of California Division of Agricultural Sciences. From start to finish the process takes about 2 weeks.

For every 2 gallons of olives you harvest, you'll need a 10- to 12-quart stoneware crock, glass container, or plastic pail. Don't use aluminum or galvanized metal. You'll also need a long-handled spoon and a cloth or old dish towel to help keep the olives submerged in the container. Making green-ripe olives

requires table salt and household lye. Lye is caustic, so to protect your hands from a lye burn, you'll need heavy-duty rubber gloves.

Begin processing the olives early in the day. The first steps take at least 12 hours and you must check the progress of the fruit frequently. As a precautionary measure, before you start, prepare a solution of 1 cup vinegar and 1 cup water to wash your skin in case it comes in contact with the lye solution. Also, for your own safety, *do not taste* the olives at any time during the lye-curing process.

The Lye Treatment:
Measuring 1 gallon of water to each 2 gallons of fruit, pour the water into the crock. Wearing rubber gloves to protect your hands, measure 1/4 cup (2 ounces) flaked or household lye for each gallon of water. Slowly pour the

lye into the water, stirring with a long-handled metal spoon until the lye dissolves. The lye heats the solution, so let it cool 30 minutes before adding the olives.

As the solution cools, cut open a few olives so you will know what the uncured flesh looks like. This way you'll have a basis for comparison when you check for lye penetration.

Slowly add the olives, being careful not to splash the lye solution. Crumple clean muslin or a dish towel and place it on top of the olives to submerge them. Exposure to air will cause green-ripe olives to darken.

Let the crock of olives stand at a temperature no higher than 60° to 70°F for 12 hours. Stir the olives with the long-handled spoon every 2 to 3 hours.

To eliminate their bitterness, olives must remain in the lye solution until the lye penetrates through the flesh to the pit. Check for penetration by cutting two or three olives of varying sizes in half. *(Be sure to wear your rubber gloves.)* Olives that are penetrated with lye will turn a dark yellow-green color. Uncured flesh will be lighter in color, more like that of the raw fruit.

If the lye has not penetrated the flesh after 12 hours, discard the lye solution and cover the olives with water. The following morning, pour off the water and cover the olives with a fresh lye solution using the same proportions of lye and water as directed above. Leave the olives in this solution until they are completely penetrated, stirring and checking them every 2 to 3 hours. This process may take up to 30 hours, depending on the variety, maturity, and size of the olives. (*Note:* It is all right if a few of the largest olives are not completely penetrated; don't discard them.)

The Rinsing Process:
Carefully pour off the lye solution and cover the fruit with cold water. Place a cloth on top of the olives, cover the container, and let the olives stand 6 hours or overnight. Thereafter, change the water daily until its color turns from a dark red to a light pink. This will take 4 to 8 days.

The Brining Process:
For each 2 gallons of fruit, prepare a weak brine of 1/2 cup table salt and 1 gallon of water. Stir to dissolve the salt. Add the olives to the brine, cover the container, and let the fruit stand for 12 hours. (It is all right to let the olives float at this point.) Drain off the brine and prepare another solution with the same proportions of salt and water given above. Leave the olives covered with brine for 1 week.

After a week the olives will be ready to eat. Remove those you plan to eat within a few days and cover them with cold water for about an hour. Then drain and serve.

For the remaining olives, replace the brine with a holding solution of 1-1/4 cups (1 pound) table salt to each gallon of water. Store the olives covered with this solution in the refrigerator for up to 6 months. After 4 months, replace the solution with fresh.

To keep olives at room temperature, prepare a heavy holding solution of 2-1/4 cups salt to each gallon of water. Store the olives, covered in this solution, up to 6 months.

Before you serve the olives, soak them in water overnight; then drain. Refrigerate leftover olives and eat them within 3 or 4 days. If at any time the olives turn mushy, moldy, or bad smelling, do not eat or even taste them. Dispose of them immediately.

INDEX